The Nature a

Catherine M. Robb

Abstract

Talents play a central role in the way that we live our lives, and it is widely assumed that identifying and developing one's talents is valuable, both for oneself and for others. Despite this, the philosophical literature is seriously lacking in its discussion of the *nature* and *value* of talent; the objective goodness of talent and its development is often assumed without an analysis of what a talent is, and the value that we place on it. This dissertation aims to provide such an analysis, offering a philosophical account of the nature and value of talent, and an account of why we value its development. In doing so, I demonstrate how this can inform and help us assess the debates and arguments that are made in the existing philosophical literature on talent. I do not aim to provide an exhaustive overview of all the philosophical issues that could be raised in relation to the value of talent and talent development, but instead I focus on three central issues that arise when analysing the nature of talents and the role that they play in our lives.

The first issue is the nature of talent itself. Here I offer an account of talent, understood as a high level of potential for a particular skill which is expressed and manifested in the excellent acquisition of that skill. The second issue is whether or not we have good prudential reasons or a moral obligation to develop our talents. I begin by objecting to Kant's claim that there is a moral duty to develop one's talents; I will argue that if there is such a duty, it will not be generated by the commitments of Kant's moral theory. I then argue that whether or not talent development is morally required, or prudentially good, is conditional on one's endorsement of the commitments that are required to bring about the development of one's talent.

Finally, I turn my focus to the relationship between talents and equality. Given the fact that some people are more talented than others, and the way in which this disrupts levels of social equality, I examine how we ought to counteract the injustice caused by unequal levels of talent. I argue that we ought to adopt the luck egalitarian neutralisation approach, as this most plausibly frames the way in which unequal talents disrupt levels of equality, and why any arising inequalities count as unjust.

Table of Contents

Abbreviations

References to works by Kant:

Anthropology: *Anthropology from a Pragmatic Point of View*

GW: *Groundwork for the Metaphysics of Morals*

MM: *The Metaphysics of Morals*

Introduction

Talents play a central role in the way that we live and organise our lives. For those who are talented, their talent allows them to more efficiently and uniquely develop a particular set of skills, and doing so can often shape their personal development, determining the choices that they make and the conception of the good life that they endorse. It is a widely accepted assumption that identifying and developing one's talents is valuable, for oneself or for others; talents are considered to directly contribute to personal flourishing, as well as contributing indirectly to the flourishing of others. Developing one's talents also has social and political implications; the resources produced and consumed by identifying and nurturing one's talents impacts on how goods are distributed in society and how social institutions are organised. Most of the time these effects are considered to be positive, allowing for a more efficient and productive functioning of society.

This positive understanding of the value of talents for individuals and society is illustrated by the recent increase in talent development programmes across educational, governmental and commercial institutions. For example, government-funded 'UK Sport' has recently launched its "biggest ever" talent identification and development programme (UK Sport 2015), whilst the national arts bodies of both England and Scotland have recently recognised talent development as a strategic priority (see Arts Council England 2017; Creative Scotland 2014). In the commercial sector, the discussion of how best to attract and manage talented employees has become increasingly fashionable, with international consulting firms such as McKinsey & Company and PwC offering services that claim to aid their clients in retaining and promoting talented employees (McKinsey & Company 2017; PwC 2017). From this it is clear that institutionalised talent identification and development programmes are a commonplace feature of most contemporary western societies, and that these programmes are thought to have positive implications.

Despite the increasing social interest in the way that talents are managed and cultivated, and the positive and central role that talents are considered to play in our lives, it is surprising to note that the philosophical literature is seriously lacking in its discussion of the nature and value of talents. Some moral theories, particularly Kant's deontology and Hurka's moral perfectionism, do make a strong connection between the value of talent development and moral agency, but this connection is based on an assumption that developing one's talents is necessarily and objectively good. A similar assumption is made in the philosophical literature on well-being; most theories of well-being include talent development as an element of what makes a person's life go well. But these claims are made without an analysis of what a talent is, the value that we place on talents and their development, and the ethical questions that arise from this. In political philosophy, talents are central to the egalitarian debate concerning how goods in society ought to be organised such that unfair advantages do not emerge from an unequal distribution of ability. Again, the debate unfolds without a substantial and systematic philosophical account of the nature of talents and why we value their development.

This dissertation aims to provide such an account, offering a philosophical analysis of the nature of talent and why we value its development, and demonstrating how this account can inform and help us assess the arguments made in the existing philosophical literature on talent. In doing so, I do not aim to provide an exhaustive overview of all the philosophical issues that could be raised in relation to talent and talent development. Instead I focus on three of the central issues that arise when analysing the nature of talents and the role that they play in our lives.

The first issue is the nature of talent itself. Here I offer an account of what a talent is, engaging with debates raised in philosophy of mind and the philosophy of psychology. Evaluating the concept of talent in this way is important because it makes clear exactly what is being analysed; this is even more pertinent given that in the literature thus far, the word 'talent' has been used ambiguously, and this ambiguity has given rise to different accounts of the value of talent that seem to talk past each other and unintentionally refer to contrasting phenomena. Once a unified account of the nature of talents is in place, this equivocation can be avoided. This is the task of Chapter One.

The second issue that I focus on is whether or not we have good prudential reasons or a moral obligation to develop our talents. We often react negatively when we hear of cases in which a person has neglected or failed to develop her talents, and it is important to understand what values ground this intuitive negative reaction. In the existing philosophical literature, the positive value of talent development is predominantly merely assumed, and this assumption is often used to ground the strong claim that there is a prudential reason or a moral obligation to develop one's talents. For example, most philosophical theories of well-being claim, either explicitly or implicitly, that the development of one's talents is prudentially good in some way; in this case, our negative reaction to wasted talents is grounded in the claim that by failing to develop one's talents, one is missing out on a prudential good. When it comes to morality, whether or not developing one's talents is considered to be morally good will usually depend on whether doing so is either allowed or required by the particular principles of the moral theory in question. For example, virtue ethics might claim that developing one's talents is morally required if doing so promotes virtuous action, or if failing to do so undermines the expression of virtue. In this way, our negative reaction to wasted talents is grounded in the claim that by failing to develop one's talents, one is failing to act morally.

There are specific theories of well-being and morality, however, that make even stronger claims than this, based on the assumption that developing one's talents represents one of the most valuable forms of human flourishing and moral development. Welfare perfectionists, for example, claim that not only is the development of one's talents prudentially valuable, but that talent development is itself a constitutive part of one's well-being, such that it is objectively and necessarily prudentially good. With regards to moral theory, both Kant and moral perfectionists explicitly claim that there is a moral obligation to develop one's talents. The reason for this moral demand is not just that it falls out of the particular principles of the moral theory, as was the case with the example of virtue ethics above, but rather that there is a necessary and fundamental connection between talent development and morality.

In Chapters Two, Three and Four I argue that we should reject the theories that make these stronger claims regarding the connection between talent development, well-being and morality. Whilst I do not deny that developing one's talents may have moral and prudential value, my claim is that (a) the prudential reasons and moral obligation to develop one's talents cannot be generated from the various commitments of the theories themselves, and (b) even if such an obligation or prudential reason could be generated by those theories, or any others, this would give rise to a particular form of the demandingness objection. This demandingness objection is grounded in the endorsement constraint, which claims that the goodness of developing one's talents is conditional on one's endorsement of the commitments that are necessary to bring about the development of one's talents. If this endorsement constraint is not met, then I argue that any theory of morality or well-being that claims the development of one's talent to be objectively good and universally constitutive of moral agency or well-being, is implausible.

The third central issue that I focus on in this dissertation is the relationship between talent and equality. One of the key debates in political philosophy has centred on the worry that institutionalised talent identification and development unjustly disrupts levels of social equality. This egalitarian concern gives rise to an axiological tension; on the one hand, we recognise the value in identifying and developing our talents, but on the other hand, doing so potentially gives rise to unjust inequalities. Given the fact of unequal talents and the worry that this poses for egalitarian justice, in the final chapter of this dissertation I examine how we ought to respond to the fact that there are unequal levels of talent in society. To do so I focus on the dominant debate in the literature between luck egalitarianism and relational egalitarianism, assessing how successfully these competing theories argue that we ought to counteract the disadvantages caused by unequal talents. I argue that luck egalitarianism offers the best response, because it most plausibly frames why unequal talents disrupt levels of equality, and why any arising inequalities count as unjust.

Before I outline the structure and chapter plan of the dissertation in more detail, let me qualify one important terminological point. In the following chapters I will often discuss the nature and grounds of the potential moral obligation we might have to develop our talents. For the purposes of this dissertation, I take an 'obligation' to be synonymous with a 'duty', so that, for example, when someone is claimed to have a moral obligation, this simply amounts to the fact that they have a moral duty. Furthermore, I assume that a moral obligation (duty) to develop one's talents arises because it is what an agent has most moral reason to do. For example, if consequentialism claims that I have a moral obligation to X, this is because doing X is morally required – it is what that particular theory of morality tells me I have most moral reason to do. And the same goes for theories of well-being; for the purposes of this dissertation I take it that the claim that X is prudentially good for an agent equates to the claim that the agent has good prudential reasons to do X.

* * *

I begin, in Chapter One, by noting that in everyday language and in the philosophical literature, there is some ambiguity about what is meant by the notion of a talent and how it differs from the closely related notions of 'ability', 'endowment', and 'capacity'. In fact, most authors use these words interchangeably. I argue that this conflation is mistaken and propose that a talent should be understood as a high level of potential for a particular skill that is manifested in the excellent acquisition and development of that particular skill. I conclude the chapter by outlining how this account of talent makes sense of some of the reasons why we value talents and their development.

In Chapter Two I focus on Kant's explicit claim that there is a moral duty to develop one's talents; I explain the arguments that ground this claim and discuss three objections that can be raised against Kant's account. First, it could be objected that Kant is mistaken when he claims that the duty to develop one's talents is an 'imperfect' duty rather than a 'perfect' one. I argue that in fact the duty to develop one's talents need not be thought of as imperfect or perfect, but as part of a continuum of stringency that can be applied to any moral duty. Second, Kant argues that the moral duty we have to develop one's talents is one that is owed specifically to oneself. However, it could be objected that the duty should only be thought of as a duty that we owe to others, and not to oneself. I argue that Kant can respond successfully to this objection. Finally, I object to Kant's claim due to the fact that he cannot generate the moral priority to develop specifically our *talents*, as opposed to any other ability or competency that we may have. In other words, there is no reason for Kant to claim that talents are more morally significant than mere competencies when it comes to developing and perfecting one's moral agency. As a result, from the commitments of his own theory, Kant cannot successfully conclude that there is a moral obligation to develop one's talents.

In Chapter Three I argue that both moral perfectionism and welfare perfectionism are equally unable to generate the claim that there is a moral obligation or prudential reason to develop one's talents. This is for two reasons. First, I object to the shared perfectionist claim that developing one's talents necessarily counts as constitutive of one's excellent human flourishing. Second, I argue that welfare perfectionism violates the 'endorsement constraint'; developing one's talent is only prudentially good for an agent if the agent endorses, or would endorse if under optimal decision-making conditions, the normative commitments that are necessarily required to bring about the development of her talent. If there is no such endorsement, then developing one's talents cannot be considered as constitutive of one's well-being or human flourishing. As a result, the commitments of both moral perfectionism and welfare perfectionism cannot successfully generate the claim that one has good prudential reasons or a moral obligation to develop one's talents.

In Chapter Four I argue that irrespective of a particular moral theory's commitments, if that theory claims there is a moral obligation to develop one's talents, then it is potentially subject to a particular form of the demandingness objection. This objection claims that if a moral obligation requires one to unreasonably sacrifice one's non-moral commitments, then it is implausibly demanding. I argue that this demandingness objection should not be formulated in terms of morality's overridingness, but instead should be based on the substantive values and commitments that come with the particular content of the moral obligation itself. I propose that when it comes to the moral obligation to develop one's talents, what counts as an unreasonable sacrifice of one's non-moral concerns is grounded in a failure to meet the endorsement constraint, such that an agent does not endorse the normative commitments that are necessary to bring about the development of her talent.

This means that the endorsement constraint I introduced in Chapter Three does not only place a condition on welfare perfectionism or any account of well-being that claims we have prudential reasons to develop our talents. The endorsement constraint also places a condition on any theory of morality that claims there is a moral obligation to develop one's talents. Therefore, if one *does* have a moral obligation to develop one's talents, it will be conditional on one's endorsement of that development, as specified by the endorsement constraint.

Even if there is a moral obligation, or there are good prudential reasons to develop one's talents, egalitarianism tells us that we ought to be sensitive to the brute fact that some people are more talented than others. Given the fact of unequal talents and the way in which this disrupts levels of social equality, in Chapter Five I examine how we ought to respond to the injustice caused by inequalities in levels of talent. I argue that we ought to adopt the luck egalitarian neutralisation approach, which aims to eradicate unjust inequalities in levels of talent, to the extent that these inequalities are a matter of bad brute luck – luck that arises due to a person's circumstances and for which she has no control.

In the conclusion I summarise, drawing together the various arguments of the previous chapters, and consider some important questions that have had to be left unanswered. In doing so, I will highlight interesting avenues for further research.

Chapter One
The Nature of Talent

1.1. Introduction

It is commonly assumed that developing one's talents is valuable and that there are good prudential and moral reasons to do so. In order to determine what reasons we may have for valuing talents and their development, and what might ground the claim that we have an obligation to develop our talents, it should be clear what we mean when we claim that someone is 'talented'. If we do have an obligation to develop our talents, or if we have reasons to find doing so valuable, then we ought to know what exactly we are to be developing, or what we claim to be valuable.

In both everyday language and in the philosophical literature, however, it is not clear what is meant by the concept of a talent, and how it differs from the closely related notions of 'ability', 'endowment', and 'capacity'. For example, Kant uses the word 'talent' as synonymous with the terms 'natural gifts' and 'capacities' (Kant GW 4:423), whilst Thomas Hurka interchangeably uses the words 'talent' and 'ability' (Hurka 1993: 15, 96). Furthermore, in the literature on distributive justice, Gerry Cohen claims that a talent is an 'inherent capacity' (Cohen 2011: 19, 30), Elizabeth Anderson refers to it as a 'native endowment' (Anderson: 302), whilst both Ronald Dworkin and John Rawls use the words 'talent', 'ability' and 'skill' as synonymous (Dworkin 2000: 92, 97; Rawls 1999: 63, 73).

Although this confusion could be dismissed as a mere terminological oversight, there is a substantive difference at stake. On the one hand, these terms could be thought of as competencies that have already been expressed and developed to some extent, and on the other hand, they could suggestive of raw potential that has yet to be expressed or cultivated. Often, the subtle difference between these concepts that are apparently synonymous with talent is also highlighted by the inclusion of the terms 'natural' or 'innate'; if something is termed as natural then it is often assumed to be an aspect of one's genetic potential, rather than something that has been shaped by one's development and environment.

The definitional ambiguity that is apparent in the literature is also echoed in the way that we seem to use the word 'talent' in everyday language. In differing circumstances we will either use the word to mean someone's innate potential, or the level of their already expressed and developed ability. For example, when we claim that the ten year-old Usain Bolt was a talented sprinter, we might be referring to his 'natural' promise or potential, such that if he developed this potential then we would predict him to be an exceptionally skilled sprinter.[1] In doing so we might pay attention to Bolt's physical and cognitive attributes; his particular body shape, determination and willingness to practice, his efficiency in picking up new techniques, and how he listens to and acts upon instruction. By calling Bolt 'talented' in this way, we have referred to his levels of potential and the capacity he has to become an excellent sprinter. By contrast, however, when labelling the young Bolt as talented we might also be referring to the fact that he is *already* highly skilled and displays an ability that is above average. He may have, for example, already won important competitions, broken records, or be able to run comparatively faster than his peers.

The two uses of the word 'talent' are separable; the first definition describes a talent as the potential for excellence *if* developed, whilst the second definition understands talent as a capacity that has already been expressed to some extent, already allowing an agent to demonstrate excellence for a particular skill. For instance, someone might possess a high level of sprinting potential, displaying the right kind of physical and mental traits to make an excellent sprinter, but have not yet received the formal training to turn that potential into excellent performance on the track. Or, a particular sprinter might have won sprinting competitions, broken records, and run faster than his peers, but at the same time have had to face considerable physical and mental challenges in doing

---

[1] For example, Ronay's recent article in *The Guardian* has described the talent of a professional footballer as a "natural gift" (Ronay 2014).

so because he is not 'naturally' disposed to be an excellent sprinter, perhaps having the wrong kind of body shape or lack of competitive spirit.

Although these two definitions can come apart, they both capture salient aspects that are apparent in our descriptions of what counts as a talent. As such, in this chapter I propose a working definition of talent that aims to incorporate and make sense of both the everyday uses of the word. A talent, I suggest, should be understood as both potential *and* excellence. If someone is talented, they will have a high level of potential for a particular skill which is manifested and expressed in the excellent acquisition and development of that skill. This means that a talent is not merely the raw potential or capacity from which we nurture certain abilities and skills, but rather it is that potential manifested in the efficient and productive acquisition of those abilities and skills. Talent is therefore the excellent expression of skill acquisition that is grounded in one's high level of potential for that skill. This means that talent is the expression of a particular skill, *and* the potential with which that skill is acquired.

In what follows I elucidate and make a case for this account of the nature of talent. Section Two will outline the reasons why we ought to consider talent as constituted by potential, understood as a dispositional quality. Section Three rejects the environmentalist account of talent, which claims that high levels of skill are not to be understood in terms of natural potential, but instead constituted by environmental stimuli and social variables. In Section Four I argue that potential ought not to be understood as merely 'natural', but that which incorporates the dynamic interaction between genetic and social factors. In Section Five I outline the reasons why potential is not enough for an account of talent; talents ought to be understood as the excellent manifestation and expression of this potential. One of the reasons for this is that what counts as a talent is determined by already-held normative judgements based on what society values as worthwhile, concerning both the level of someone's skill and the domain of that skill. This means that the positive judgement involved in evaluating someone as talented is contextual; comparative and relative to cultural norms and values. I conclude in Section Six by outlining how my account of talent initially allows us to make sense of why we value talents and their development.

Before continuing to the next section, I would like to be clear about the reason for focusing on forming an account of the nature of talent. It could be argued that for the purpose of engaging with the substantive normative questions I raise in later chapters, I only need to identify and use as a point of departure the definition of talent that is most commonly used, or most relevant to, the existing moral and political literature. In that case I would only need to stipulate a definition of talent that works specifically for the moral and political issues that will arise in the proceeding chapters. After all, if Kant means 'natural potential' when he uses the word 'talent', then his claim that we have a moral obligation to develop our talents simply means that we have a moral obligation to develop our natural potential. In order to analyse the substantive philosophical points, it may be sufficient to merely accept and understand what each author means by their use of the word.

However, as I have already highlighted, it is unclear by referring to the literature and our everyday use of the word, what a talent actually is and what authors mean by their use of the word. By stipulating one interpretation over another, I would be neglecting an aspect of talent that some authors have deemed to be significant. Furthermore, my aim in this dissertation is not merely to internally critique various philosophers' arguments, but to unearth whether their claims about the moral and political implications that arise from talents and their development are plausible. To answer the question whether we have an obligation to develop our talents, or whether there are good prudential reasons to do so, it is vitally important to understand what a talent is. And in order for the answer to have any significant wider import, the understanding of talent that I use has to ring true and pick out essential features of the phenomenon.

As such, the definition of talent cannot simply be stipulated, but argued for, by putting up for scrutiny the ways in which we use the term in everyday language and in the philosophical literature, so as to arrive at and prescribe a less ambiguous and more useful definition of talent than the relatively confused one that is currently on offer. In doing so, I propose an account of talent that psychologists Sternberg and Davidson call 'implicit', attempting to theorise the conceptual question about the nature of talent, rather than analysing the cognitive or physical capacities that are present in a person who is already labelled as 'talented' (Sternberg & Davidson 1986: 10).[2]

1.2. Potential as a Dispositional Quality

The account of talent that I propose in this chapter is one that incorporates both the notions of potential and excellence. A talent is, I claim, a high level of potential for a skill that is excellently manifested in the ease and speed with which that particular skill is acquired and developed. In this section I discuss why 'potential' must feature as a necessary condition when defining the nature of talent.

Potential is not only a necessary pre-requisite for being talented, but is also necessary for being able to develop any skill, no matter how trivial we might deem it to be. It seems impossible, not just unlikely, that someone or something will be able to achieve X, or be X, without having the potential to achieve or be X. This potential can be understood as a dispositional quality, which as Gilbert Ryle has argued, does not require an agent or object "to be in a particular state, or to undergo a particular change, [but...] to be bound or liable to be in a particular state, or to undergo a particular change, when a particular change is realized" (Ryle: 31). For example, in terms of inanimate objects, a piece of wood has the potential to become furniture in virtue of its disposition to be carved in a particular way, and a glass can be broken in virtue of the disposition of fragility, which results in it shattering when hit under the right circumstances. When it comes to the potential for humans to behave or act in a certain way, it is clear that without the relevant dispositions, such actions or behaviours would be impossible. For example, in order to play tennis a person has to have the relevant dispositions to be able to hold the racket, throw and hit the ball, and to move

---

[2] This latter type of theory is what is called an "explicit" theory of talent, focussing on the "internal" and "cognitive" processes that are involved in understanding how talented people function in their specific skill domains (Sternberg & Davidson 1986: 10). Renzulli's (2005) "three-ring" conception of talent is an example of an explicit theory, claiming that talented individuals show a higher level of ability, task commitment and creativity.

around the court. In order to sing there is an initial dispositional requirement to be able to move one's vocal chords and to control the sound or vibrations that are emitted from them.[3]

When we refer to someone as having the kind of potential that counts as a talent, however, we are not merely referring to the basic dispositions that are needed for any of our behaviours and actions to arise. For example, we consider a glass to be *more* fragile, *more* disposed to break, if it is structured in a particular way. We can even compare the fragility of different glasses – one glass is more fragile than another if it displays the relevant dispositional qualities more than the other glass. By analogy, we consider an agent as being disposed to play tennis better than others, the more she displays the relevant dispositional qualities; for example, that she is *more* disposed to have the right kind of body shape, quick reflexes, good co-ordination, and is able to move with agility around the court. And so, the high level of potential in those who are talented are qualities that dispose them, upon development of a particular skill, to acquire and develop that skill with more ease and speed (Gagné 1998: 416). This does not imply that those who do not have high levels of potential are precluded from attaining expert performance, but rather that someone who has a high level of potential for a particular skill will find the development of that skill to come with more ease and precociousness.

Take for example a comparative case of two sprinters: sprinter *A* and sprinter *B*. Both sprinters have reached the same level of success, running the same exceptionally fast time for the 100m race. However, *A* has found sprinting more of a challenge – he has had to practice longer hours, adapt his diet, receive more guidance from his teachers, and spend more time in the gym to change his

---

[3] In order to avoid certain objections that can be raised against dispositional accounts of ability, such as the 'finkish' objection raised by Martin (1994) and the 'masking' objection raised by Choi (2012), I suggest that for sake of argument we assume Michael Fara's account of dispositions, specifying that a disposition will be manifested only under the relevant conditions: "An agent has the ability to *A* in circumstances *C* if and only if she has the disposition to *A* when, in circumstances *C*, she tries to *A*" (Fara 2008: 848). As such, an agent's or object's external environment may mask a disposition's manifestation, but not *remove* the disposition altogether. For a discussion on the relationship between dispositions and manifestation conditions, see Stephen Mumford's (1998) realist account of dispositions.

body shape. Sprinter *B*, on the other hand, has found that the sport comes quite easily to him – he has had to practice much less than *A*, hardly spends any time training with his coach, and spends half the time in the gym compared to *A*. On my account of talent, it is sprinter *B* who has higher levels of potential, determined by the amount of effort that needs to be invested in the development of his skill. Given the same level of skill, a person who needs to invest more effort in developing that skill is considered to have less potential than the person who invests less effort.

According to the account of talent I have been sketching so far, a talent is a high level of potential, understood as a dispositional quality manifested in a particular way; if someone is talented then they will be disposed to develop a skill with more ease and speed than someone who is not talented.[4] There is widespread assumption in the literature that these high levels of potential indexed to those who are talented are something 'natural' or 'innate', such that one's level of potential is determined genetically in some way. This is not merely assumed in the philosophical literature, but also in the field of psychology, where Howe *et al.* note the traditional picture of talent rests on an assumption of "inborn attributes" and "natural aptitudes" that are explanatory and predictive of future success (Howe *et al.* 1998: 399).

However, the scientific evidence that would be needed to determine whether a person's dispositions are 'innate' in this way is inconclusive. Some psychologists worry that it might be ethically problematic to empirically assess whether talents stem from purely genetic potential. Trehub and Schellenburg, for instance, have concerns that the experiments needed to determine this would be invasive and inappropriate, requiring the researcher to programme "the lives of

---

[4] It is important to note that even though a talent is expressed in the ease and speed with which a skill is developed, this does not mean that the skill itself will have anything to do with ease or speed. For example, it might be that someone has a disposition to be a good chess player or memorise poetry, and these skills are characterised not by speed or efficiency, but by one's level of potential for reflection and patience. My claim is just that the acquisition of the skill will come more *naturally* to the talented person, such that she finds that the reflective capacities and patience required to become a good chess player, for instance, will come more easily and require less effort than someone who is not talented.

talented children so that all potentially relevant environmental factors could be controlled" (Trehub & Schellenburg 1998: 428). Because these experiments would be ethically problematic, it is highly unlikely that they could ever be comprehensively or successfully carried out.

From the experiments that have been conducted, what has been shown is that when it comes to human development there is no such thing as a genetic disposition that is unmediated by one's social environment (Fishkin: 94). Due to the fact one's development is so influenced and mediated by one's social and physical environments, some psychologists have gone so far as to claim that what we usually think of as a talent does not exist, and instead our high levels of achievement are not determined by dispositional qualities but the manifestation of advantageous environmental stimuli, such as good teaching, parenting and hard-work. For ease of reference, this position can be called 'environmentalism'. If the environmentalist position is correct, and talents are not considered to be levels of personal dispositional qualities, then this directly refutes the account of talent I propose in this chapter. As such, before I go on to argue that potential is a necessary but not sufficient condition for a definition of talent, in the next section I will outline the environmentalist position in greater detail and offer arguments to reject it.

1.3. Against Environmentalism

The environmentalist position with regards to talents and their development has been most explicitly argued for by two groups of experimental psychologists, one headed by Michael J. Howe in the United Kingdom, and the other by K. Anders Ericsson in the United States of America. The experiments conducted by both groups have provided similar results, allowing Howe and Ericsson to conclude that talents, understood as a person's innate or natural potential, do not exist. Instead, what we originally considered to be a person's talent is instead the level of ability and skill that one accumulates as a result of advantageous environmental and social factors. In this section I will focus my discussion of the environmentalist position on Howe *et al.'s* (1998) feature article in *Behavioural and Brain Sciences*,[5] which analyses evidence collected from two of their previous empirical studies, and has subsequently stimulated much of the debate regarding environmentalism about talents.

Although Howe's article and the studies supporting it were published around twenty years ago, the findings and conclusions are still relevant for two reasons. First, developmental psychologist Françoys Gagné has recently published an article accusing environmentalists of "scholarly misconduct", claiming that they adhere to questionable research ethics and ignore evidence in their studies that seems to refute their own position (Gagné 2013: 216). Although this might seem like an *ad hominem* attack, Gagné's objection legitimately questions the integrity of the conclusions that are reached from the environmentalists' experiments, and the contemporaneity of the objection shows that the results of the relevant experiments are still up for scrutiny.

Second, the conclusions that the environmentalists reach from their experiments have recently influenced the mainstream, everyday understanding of talent. For example, in the build-up to the 2014 Commonwealth Games in Glasgow, Sport Scotland produced media explaining that being talented is a matter of enjoyment, belief and hard work; it was claimed that talent involves mostly choice and effort rather than a disposition for a specific skill (Sport Scotland 2013). There is also an increasing acceptance in the pop-science literature claiming that talents are not a matter of natural potential, but rather emerge as a result of the correct methods of practice and teaching (see Coyle 209; Colvin 2008). But, as I will now go on to show, the evidence behind these claims is inconclusive, and at most only demonstrate that we cannot ignore environmental stimuli when it comes to the development of talent. The evidence cannot be interpreted as proving that natural potential does not exist or has no part in constituting what a talent is.

Howe argues that talents, understood as emerging from natural potential, do not exist, and that the ease and speed with which people acquire different

---

[5] From hereon I will omit the '*et al.*' from this reference.

skills is not explained by natural potential, but is rather the product of environmental factors (Howe *et al.* 1998: 401). There are four main arguments offered for this environmentalist account: (i) the environmentalist account is more socially acceptable, (ii) anti-environmentalist reasoning about talent is circular, (iii) the anthropological evidence counts in favour of environmentalism, and (iv) the evidence from empirical studies counts in favour of environmentalism. I will now outline and respond to each of these arguments in turn.

(i) Howe argues that the environmentalist position has more desirable, positive social implications than an account of talent that emphasises dispositional qualities. Howe's claim is that categorising people as having natural potential is "unfair", "discriminatory" and "wasteful"; those who are not deemed as having natural potential are often refused resources and denied the educational encouragement that is needed to succeed (ibid., 399, 407). To pump our intuitions, Howe asks us to imagine the unfairness of limiting resources and encouragement for key school subjects such as mathematics and language skills, to those who are labelled by their schools as having natural potential. Surely, those who are not naturally disposed to be highly skilled in those subjects require the same amount of, if not more, resources and encouragement in order to progress and succeed. By admitting that natural potential does not exist, Howe claims that fairer and more equal allocations of resources and opportunities can be made (ibid., 436).

However, this argument from negative social implications is misguided because it does not show that there are no natural differences in levels of potential. Just because it might be unfair to distribute resources according to levels of potential, this does not mean that no such difference exists. We might think, for example, that allocating resources on the basis of skin colour is unfair and morally wrong, but this does not demonstrate that there is no such difference in skin colour. Just because there might be a tension between talent identification and discrimination, this does not mean that we have good reasons to reject the understanding of a talent as emerging from a person's own level of potential (Winner 1998: 431). Howe's intuition pump only serves to make explicit the importance of further philosophical consideration into the social, moral and political implications that arise with regards to talents and their development. I go on to discuss these moral and political implications throughout the proceeding chapters of this dissertation.

(ii) Howe argues that appealing to the notion of natural potential to explain high levels of skill acquisition and achievement results in circular reasoning. The circularity can be stated as follows: we claim that someone's high level of achievement for playing a musical instrument, for example, stems from their talent understood as natural potential, yet when asking how we know that they are talented (that they have natural potential) we appeal to their high level of achievement in playing their instrument. In so doing we assume natural potential as explanatory for why a person excels at a particular skill, but the only way that we know someone has natural potential for that skill is to acknowledge the demonstration of their high achievement (Howe *et al.* 1998: 405). In other words, we are using a person's level of natural potential to explain their demonstrated ability, and using their demonstrated ability to explain their level of natural potential.

There are four reasons why the explanatory circle that Howe presents does not refute the non-environmentalist position. First, Howe over simplifies the non-environmentalist account, which does not claim that *all* instances of above-average levels of skill are a result of natural potential; in some cases it might be that hard-work and good teaching explains why someone has reached a high level of skill. We do not always need to use natural potential to explain the emergence of achievement. Second, we do not necessarily have to appeal to the demonstration of high achievement to know whether someone has natural potential for that skill; it is often the case that experts in a field are able to observe a person engaging in sometimes unrelated tasks to determine whether they have high levels of natural potential for the relevant skill. Third, even if Howe was correct about the apparent circularity in reasoning, it would similarly cause problems for his own environmentalist account. As an environmentalist we could claim that someone's high level of achievement was a result of their advantageous social and environmental stimuli, yet at the same time we would only know if that person was subject to advantageous social and environmental stimuli if they demonstrated high levels of achievement.

Finally, the environmentalist's charge of circularity confuses metaphysical and epistemic claims about talent identification. One 'horn' of the dilemma seems to be a claim about how we can *know* that someone has a high level of potential, and the other 'horn' of the dilemma is a claim about what it is for someone to actually have high levels of potential, irrespective of whether we identify them as such. But there is no need to answer one horn of the dilemma in terms of the other, as Howe seems to do. In so doing, Howe confuses the epistemological question about how we can identify high levels of potential with the metaphysical question of what it is for someone to have that potential in the first place.

Take as an analogous example the virtue of kindness: I might identify and subsequently come to know that you are kind-hearted because I see you demonstrating your kindness by helping the homeless on Christmas morning. But what it is to be kind is not explained by this epistemic claim, but rather by the metaphysical claim that kindness is just the manifested disposition to help those who are in need. What it is to be kind is explained, at least in part, in terms of one's dispositional qualities, and identifying kindness is explained in terms of how we assess the manifestation of these dispositional qualities. There is no problematic tension between these metaphysical and epistemic claims. The same goes for talents: I might identify that you are talented because I witness and assess your demonstration of high levels of musical potential, but what it is to have high levels of musical potential is explained metaphysically, at least partly, in terms of your dispositional qualities. There is no explanatory circle lurking in this account.

(iii) In support of the environmentalist position Howe cites the evidence of anthropological studies suggesting that there are some cultures in which high achievement in certain skills is relatively common, whilst in other cultures achievement in those same skills is comparatively rare. For example, certain non-Western cultures are more likely to be musically accomplished than other cultures, some tribal cultures show high levels of ability in land and maritime navigation, whilst Australian Aborigines have been shown to perform more effectively at visual memory tasks. Howe claims that these cross-cultural differences and propensities in ability are a result of social learning habits and "traditional training customs", rather than individual genetic potential (ibid., 404-5).

It may be that some cultures are more likely than others to produce individuals who succeed in certain skills – the evidence of the cited anthropological studies seems to point in favour of this conclusion. However, these cultural differences do not rule out the contribution of natural potential to skill acquisition; it may be that children in certain cultures are born with a similar genetic constitution that gives rise to high levels of potential for a particular skill. The anthropological evidence is inconclusive on this matter; the prolific skills in question might be the result of dispositional qualities that are shared by the culture, rather than merely a result of the learning habits that are determined by the particular cultural environment.

(iv) Howe further offers the results of his own empirical research, purporting to demonstrate that high levels of skill acquisition are not a result of a person's dispositional qualities, but rather their environmental stimuli. I argue, however, that Howe is unjustified in drawing these environmentalist conclusions from the experiments. For the purposes of the discussion in this chapter, I will focus on one of the largest and most recent of the experiments conducted, the results of which were published in two articles, 'Are There Early Childhood Signs of Musical Ability?' (Howe *et al.* 1995), and 'The Role of Practice in the Development of Performing Musicians' (Sloboda *et al.* 1996).[6] First I will explain the experiment, and then go on to critically analyse the conclusions drawn from the findings as published in both the 1995 and 1996 articles.

The experiment conducted by Howe studied a large group of 257 music students and their parents, with regards to how environmental factors such as practice habits, quality of teaching and early musical experiences affected the students' musical development. The students were interviewed, and a sub-set of the students were also asked to complete a diary in which they documented how much practice they completed over the course of forty-two weeks. The authors

---

[6] Again, for ease of reference, I will from hereon omit the '*et al.*' from the citations of both of these articles.

divided the students into five groups depending on their musical ability; Group One consisted of children who attended Chetham's School of Music, a prestigious private music school in Manchester, Group Two consisted of children who had applied but failed to gain a place at Chetham's, Group Three's students had enquired about attending Chetham's but had not yet applied, Group Four consisted of children who attended a state school and were receiving lessons on their musical instrument, and finally, Group Five consisted of children who had previously learnt a musical instrument but had dropped out of music lessons before the study took place. The musical ability of these groups was assumed to descend with the group numbers, with Group One considered to be the most musically accomplished, as they had gained a place at a specialist music school, and Group Five considered to be the least musically accomplished.

For the sake of argument it will be useful to allow Howe his assumption about the levels of musical ability correlating with the various group numbers. However, it could be argued that the students in Groups Three and Four (those who had not yet applied to Chetham's, or who attended a non-specialist music school) were more musically able than those in Group Two, who applied to Chetham's but did not get in. It may be that those in Groups Three and Four *were* good enough to be accepted into Chetham's even though they had not yet or would not apply.

The results published in Howe's 1995 article focus on the relation between musical achievement and early signs of musical potential in the participants; Howe concludes that there is "little or no support for the view that very early signs of unusual musicality are at all common in individuals who eventually become accomplished musicians" (Howe *et al*. 1995: 163). Instead, Howe claims that early signs of musical achievement are in fact a result of environmental factors and early childhood exposure to musical activity. To demonstrate this, the parents of the students were each asked whether they had noticed any early musical behaviours in their children with regards to five different categories: singing, rhythmic movement, the liking of musical sounds, attentiveness to musical sounds, and spontaneous requests to be involved in musical activities (Ibid., 166).

With four out of the five categories, there was no difference between the groups in the age or propensity at which the children demonstrated musical behaviours. However, with regards to singing, Group One was found to be forty percent more likely to demonstrate this behaviour at an earlier age than the other groups, being almost six months ahead in development compared to the other children. Despite initially entertaining the idea that Group One's early singing propensity could be a result of differences in natural potential, Howe suggests that the age at which the child first sang is correlated to the age at which parents first began initiating musical activities. As such, the early sign of musical activity demonstrated by the child's singing ability is not due to natural potential but rather early musical experiences initiated by the child's environment (ibid., 172-3).

If this conclusion is to hold, Howe needs to prove that Group One showed a higher level of parent-initiated musical activity before the child begins to demonstrate early singing propensity. However, when parents were asked the age of the child at which they first initiated musical activity, Group One were not the youngest: Groups One, Two and Four were sung to by their parents at the same age, Group Two had parents who first moved and listened to music with them, and the parents of Groups Two and Five began musical play with their children at the youngest age. Howe acknowledges these results, claiming that "there initially appears to be little evidence that the most competent group experienced specific individual parent-initiated behaviours at an earlier age than the other groups" (ibid., 174). It is therefore hard to see why Howe concludes without reservation that the early signs of singing ability are a result of early musical exposure. The results could equally have been caused by the fact that the children who showed earlier signs of singing ability had higher levels of musical potential, understood as an innate dispositional quality.

Sloboda's analysis of the experimental data in his 1996 article focusses on the tight relationship between practice and the development of musical ability, concluding that formal practice is "a fundamental causal agent in skill acquisition rather than merely a covariate of it" (Sloboda *et al.* 1996: 289-290). The data of the study seems to demonstrate that high amounts of practice result in high levels of musical achievement, even before increases in parental and teacher involvement in the child's musical development. This correlation was claimed by Sloboda to be direct, such that "[h]igh achievers practice the most, moderate achievers practice a moderate amount, and low achievers practice hardly at all" (ibid., 306). In the first year of playing their instrument, all the groups reported that they engaged in roughly fifteen to twenty minutes of practice each day, but by the time the students had been playing for four years, Group One increased to forty-five minutes of practice per day, Groups Two and Three increased to twenty-five minutes per day, and Groups Four and Five showed no change over time (ibid., 296-7). The evidence was taken to demonstrate that as the students continued to progress throughout the years of their musical development, Group One ended up doing significantly more practice than the other groups, and as such, this resulted in higher musical achievement. This means that the level of student practice time appears directly correlative to their level and demonstration of musical ability.

The study further emphasises this connection by deciding upon a child's level of musical achievement based on which 'grade' the students managed to achieve in the Associated Board of Music and Drama exams, of which there are eight possible grades, with eight denoting the highest achievement. The study found that Group One progressed to grades three or four by the fourth year of their instrumental training, whilst Groups Two to Five had only progressed, at the most, to grade two. The mean hours of practice between the passing of grade exams was calculated, and Sloboda found that there was no significant difference between the groups: "[i]t took the same number of hours of practice to achieve a given grade level, regardless of which group participants belonged to" (ibid., 300). Therefore, Sloboda concludes that practice is shown to correlate directly and explain musical achievement; Group One achieved a higher grade due to their practicing almost twice as much as the other groups, whilst the other groups achieved a lower grade level due to their practicing almost less than half as Group One.

However, the conclusions that Sloboda reaches in the 1996 article are mistaken for two reasons. First, Sloboda does not convincingly give evidence for the claim that practice is a fundamental causal factor in the explanation of musical development. This is particularly evident when asking *why* the students practiced the amounts that they did; seeing as each group initially started practicing for the same amount of time, it might have been the case that Group One – the 'excellent' group – were motivated to engage in more practice time due to a realisation that they had natural potential. This natural potential might have allowed them to see quicker and more efficient results from their practice, or allowed them to enjoy their playing more, thus motivating them to engage in more practice time.

Furthermore, Group One attended a specialist music school that sets dedicated practice time as part of the school day; the amount of practice time for Group One occurred as a result of the student being accepted to the school in the first place. The hours of practice for each student who attended Chetham's was therefore dictated and determined by the fact that they demonstrated a high enough level of ability to be accepted to the school. Acceptance into a specialist music school depends on the teachers of the school recognising musical ability in the student, and this ability may arise as a result of environmental factors and social circumstances, but the evidence does not rule out this ability could also have been a result of the student's own natural potential. As such, Sloboda still has a burden of proof to demonstrate that the correlation between practice and musical achievement is not caused by natural potential.

The second reason why Sloboda's conclusion is mistaken is that the experiment itself was not designed to highlight differences in the *quality* but only the *quantity* of the practice and achievement. Assessing achievement based on the passing of an Associated Board exam does not distinguish carefully enough between the quality of a performance; passing the exam with a 'distinction' – the highest mark – is very different to passing it with the lowest mark of a 'pass'. With this in mind, it could be the case that with the same level and amount of practice, the students in Group One were receiving much higher marks in their exams, which can only be shown if we look to the quality of the pass marks and the quality of the time spent practicing. There is nothing in the experimental evidence, therefore, to rule out that this difference in quality may be a result of a difference in natural potential, understood as a dispositional quality. Without taking into consideration the quality of the musicianship, the findings of the study are unable to discount natural potential as a causal factor for musical excellence, let alone prove that practice and encouragement are direct determining causal factors.[7]

Therefore, the experimental evidence for environmentalism is inconclusive; the evidence does not provide the data to rule out that high levels of achievement could be caused by natural potential. In the next section, I argue that there is a reason for this inconclusiveness: the experimental evidence cannot rule out natural potential over environmentalism because one's dispositional qualities arise as a dynamic interaction between both genetic constitution and environmental stimuli. As a result, we do not need to forgo the claim that talents are constituted by levels of potential. Instead, when we claim that a talent is a high level of potential for a particular skill, that potential is not solely genetically determined nor solely determined by environmental factors, but is constituted by the interaction between both one's genes and one's environment. In this respect, we have to reject environmentalism; it is not the case that talents, understood as potential for a particular skill, do not exist.

1.4. Not just *Natural* Potential

The support for environmentalism stems from the attractive claim that environmental and social stimuli play an important causal role in the development of ability. However, this intuition and the evidence that is cited to support it, does not rule out the equally important contribution of a person's genetic constitution. The claim that both genetic *and* environmental factors contribute to a person's development is not new; it has long been the norm in the field of

---

[7] In a later article, Howe admits that the results of this experiment cannot rule out natural potential as being a causal factor for musical excellence; he states that "there exist no findings which conclusively rule out genetic contributions to individual differences in musical achievement. We have never asserted otherwise. On the other hand, we are aware of no findings which make it necessary or inevitable to accept that specific observed differences are caused by genetic factors" (Sloboda *et al.* 1999: 53). This concession is still rather uncharitable, however, seeing as some of the evidence in the experiment *does* point to significant differences in musical achievement as being caused by what might be thought of as natural potential.

epigenetics to accept that one's genetic make-up and one's environment are dynamically interconnected, such that they cannot be said to play two distinctly separate causal roles in one's development. Whilst one's environment allows genes to express themselves in various ways, it is also the case that one's environmental stimuli play a definitive role in how genes are formed and transformed (Fishkin: 86-89; Beck *et al.* 1999; Eckhardt *et al.* 2004; Weinhold 2006).[8]

To demonstrate this, scientific studies have shown that genetic formation in foetal development is in part causally determined in relation to the mother's behaviour and environmental circumstances. For example, extra stress levels in the mother can affect the formation of the genes that control brain function, and children born during a famine are more likely to store sugars more readily than others, thus resulting in a higher propensity to develop obesity and diabetes in later years of life (Fishkin: 115).

Genetic modification due to environmental factors does not only occur during foetal development, but also throughout a person's life into adulthood. For example, prolonged periods of stress in adults has been shown to reduce to the size of the hippocampus which affects levels of memory retention, and people experiencing poverty have been shown to be more likely to form a smaller prefrontal cortex, which can affect executive functioning and the capacity to make long-term decisions (ibid.). In these cases, genetic code is not merely expressed, but is adapted and formed in response to one's surrounding environment; one's environment directly constitutes one's genetic dispositions and the way these dispositions are expressed.

Because development occurs as an interaction between genetic make-up and environmental stimuli, the dispositional qualities that are exhibited when

---

[8] Just because it is inaccurate or epistemically challenging to decipher which part of one's development is caused by one's genetic constitution or one's environment due to the close interaction between both these elements, it is not necessarily the case that these two elements are metaphysically indistinct. In this chapter I make no such claim, and leave aside the question of whether the dynamic interaction between genetic and environmental factors render the metaphysical distinction between them less robust than originally thought.

someone is talented should not be understood as merely 'natural' or 'innate' potential, as is so often assumed in the literature. This is because we cannot merely accept that a person is born with a determined level of genetic potential and that the structure of society merely allows that talent to express itself. Instead, the disposition of the talented individual to acquire a skill with ease and speed is generated by a dynamic and constant interaction between her genetic constitution and her environmental inputs, both before and after birth. This means that by the time we initially identify and assess one's level of potential for a particular skill, there will have already been normatively significant social and environmental interactions that affect one's genetic dispositions and one's subsequent level of potential for the skill in question. As such, the fact that there are different levels of talent amongst individuals in society also points to the fact that people have experienced different levels of formative developmental experiences in their social environment.

Given the importance of environmental and social factors for the formation of talents, in Chapter Five I discuss in more detail the implications that arise due to unequal levels of talent and how we ought to provide equal social opportunities for talent identification and development. In the next section of this chapter, however, I will argue that potential by itself is not sufficient for a plausible account of what a talent is. In doing so I refute Howe's rejection of natural potential but at the same time accommodate his claim that environmental stimuli are vital for the development of one's capacities. I argue that in fact environmental stimuli plays a necessary and constituent role in the development of one's capacities.

1.5. Talents as Potential *and* Excellence

Understanding talent as a high level of potential for a particular skill is not sufficient for a plausible and comprehensive account of the nature of talent. A talent cannot just be a certain amount of potential for a skill, or a certain kind of dispositional quality. Instead, a talent is the expression of one's level of potential, manifested in the way that one excellently develops a particular skill with efficiency and precociousness. This means that a talent is performative and domain-specific, in the way that psychologist Feldman proposes (Feldman 1986: 302).

The way in which talents are performative is analogous to the way that we understand the nature of virtue. In virtue theory, it is not merely the disposition for virtuous action that determines whether an agent is virtuous, but that she also needs to express and demonstrate this disposition as virtuous *action*. A person is not deemed virtuous, then, until her disposition is manifested and expressed; being virtuous is just acting in such a way that is appropriate to the specific situation that one finds oneself in – virtue requires action in a particular context (Zagzebski 1996: 113-116, 130-135). For example, the virtue of courage does not only require that one is disposed to act courageously, but that this disposition is acted upon in the appropriate way that is required by the situation. Without this actualisation, an agent is merely *disposed* to be virtuous, rather than being virtuous itself.

I do not claim that talents are to be considered as virtues, but only that an analogy can be made: similarly to the virtues, talents are only talents insofar as they are the actualisation and expression of high levels of potential, realised through the acquisition of a particular skill. It is only when actually acquiring a skill that one's level of potential can be manifested as particularly indexed to that skill. Without the manifestation of one's high level of potential *for* a particular skill, one is merely disposed to be talented, rather than talented itself.[9]

Take the example of the talented British tennis player, Andy Murray. At the age of five, Murray may have had a high level of potential for playing tennis; he may have had the right height and body shape, the ability to move his body with more accurate coordination, or show higher levels of competitive spirit. However, it is only when he expresses and directs this potential to playing tennis itself, by

---

[9] Note that my claim regarding talents as constituted by one's level of potential *and* that potential as it is manifested, only refers specifically to talents. I am not making the wider claim that all instances of ability are necessarily indexed to the actual manifestations of dispositional qualities. I merely argue that *talents* must at some point be *exercised* in terms of skill acquisition.

holding a racket, running on the court, throwing and hitting balls accurately according to the rules of the game, that Murray can be said to have a talent *for* tennis. His potential is only realised as a talent for tennis once he begins to express and convert his potential in a particular way, indexed to the particular skill of playing tennis. It is the combination of Murray's high level of potential and the realisation of this potential through excellent skill acquisition that renders him a talented tennis player. Even though Murray may have already begun to develop his skill, when we claim that he has a talent, we are describing the quality of what he is *able* to achieve through the expression of his potential, and the ease with which he has already begun to actualise his skill. In this way, we acknowledge that Murray's tennis-playing ability can continuously be enhanced and developed in ways that are above-average and to an exceptionally high level.

If this were not the case, and a talent was merely a disposition, then we could claim that Murry has a talent for playing tennis even though he had never touched a tennis racket or played a game of tennis. This would be implausible for both epistemological and metaphysical reasons; not only would we be unable to *know* that Murray was talented, but there would be no fact of the matter about the way in which Murray's disposition is expressed in the acquisition of a particular skill for playing tennis. If a talent wasn't partly a performative concept in the way that I have just described, then this would have strange implications for what would count as a talent. For example, we don't think that beauty, height or body shape are talents, but rather the way in which a person uses their height, body shape, and maybe even beauty, for the excellent acquisition of a particular skill, such as basketball or tennis. As such, a talent cannot just be a dispositional quality, as this would render certain dispositional qualities as talents, when it would be implausible for this to be the case.

The case for talent to be understood as an expressive phenomenon is made even stronger by the fact that talents are comparative; to label someone as talented is to make a judgement about their skill acquisition as being of an exceptionally high level, or 'above average'. In order to assess the merits of someone's level of skill acquisition, it is therefore necessary to contrast and compare these levels to that of others. Determining what counts as a talent therefore involves acknowledging a threshold which includes within it those who have the highest levels of skill acquisition in a particular skill domain. Often that threshold will only allow for a small percentage of the comparison class to be included (Seel 2012: 3262), and the way in which we make these comparisons and determine the relevant thresholds is relative to already existing social and cultural values.

For example, when it comes to determining the level of talent attributed to children with high intelligence, the threshold is determined according to the society's or school's specific educational policy; in the United Kingdom, Terman originally suggested in 1925 that being academically talented should designate being in the first percentile of intellectual ability (Winner 2000: 153), whilst in Korea and Taiwan, by contrast, a child is determined as talented if they are two standard deviations above the average level for the age group, which is roughly equal to being in the fifth percentile (Csikszentmihalyi 1998: 411). Being talented, therefore, is determined based on where your level of skill acquisition sits within the relevant group of your peers, and the country or institution in which you are developing your skill.

Talents are not only socially determined with regards to the comparative judgements of what counts as excellent or an above average level of skill acquisition, but also with regards to the value that is placed upon particular skills. Because a talent is potential that is manifested and expressed in the acquisition of a particular skill, it requires there to be an appropriate and available way in which to express that potential. Andy Murray, for example, could not be classed as a talented tennis player if tennis was not valued in such a way as to be available in the culture or society in which he was developing his initial level of high potential.

Csikszentmihalyi provides an example that elucidates this point further. He imagines the invention of a new game called 'Mo'. In order to be able to play Mo well, one needs to be able to "recognize fine spatial and color distinctions, one must be very agile, and one must have a high tolerance for alcohol"

(Csikszentmihalyi 2015: 32).[10] Over time, Mo becomes an extremely popular game, so much so that players of Mo are revered for their abilities and paid handsome salaries. In this case, Csikszentmihalyi claims that we need to accept talent in Mo as both naturally and culturally determined: "[s]hould we concede that talent in *mo* was caused by physiological factors? Certainly, because all the component skills depend on demonstrably neurological processes. Or should we say that talent in *mo* is culturally constituted? Certainly, because the combination of physiological skills was meaningless before the game was invented" (ibid., 32). Without the value placed on Mo such that it is on offer in our society and the talented person could develop their skills accordingly, the potential needed in order to excel in Mo could not be expressed or manifested, and is consequently unable to be compared to other levels of potential and skill acquisition.

Talent is therefore both a metaphysical and epistemological phenomenon; it describes the fact that someone has, indexed to them, a personal dispositional quality that is manifested and expressed in the acquisition of a particular skill or domain. But what counts as 'excellent' is relatively derived. A good example of this is how we are able to make sense of the difference between talented Olympic swimmers and talented Paralympic swimmers: if swimming talent was defined by a set of rigid and fixed metaphysical dispositional qualities, then Paralympic swimmers might not be classed as talented, irrespective of how quickly and easily they acquire the relevant skills. However, even though Paralympic swimmers possess different dispositional qualities, and may compete with slower race times than Olympic swimmers, we can still judge certain Paralympic swimmers as 'talented', because we differently determine the comparison class and thresholds, and consequently regard the achievements of those within these different thresholds as equally valuable in our culture.

The definition of talent that I propose incorporates both of the everyday understandings of the word as potential *and* excellence. A talent is defined as the excellent acquisition of a particular skill, but this excellence is grounded in a person's high level of potential, understood as a dispositional quality. This

---

[10] Although Csikszentmihalyi does not state this explicitly, the game he describes basically sounds a lot like General Pool.

disposition is formed through a dynamic interaction between one's genetic constitution and one's environment. As a result, being talented does not merely consist in having a disposition to excellently acquire a particular skill, but also requires the manifestation of that disposition; a talent is the expression of one's dispositional qualities.[11]

Before concluding, it is important to reply to two objections that could be raised against the understanding of the nature of talent that I have just proposed. First of all, it could be objected that considering a talent as comparative and relative to the culture in which one's potential is being expressed is implausible, due to the fact that it places too much emphasis on talent as a performative and epistemological phenomenon. Surely, it could be claimed, a talent ought to be a metaphysical, dispositional quality, independent of how others' normative judgements sit in comparison.

In order to respond to this worry, consider an example of a world in which there exists only one human being, and this world is without society, culture and community. Despite this, the one person that does exist in this world finds that she has, for whatever reason, high levels of musical potential. Consequently, throughout her life she fashions make-shift musical instruments and expresses her musical potential in an excellent way. The question is whether we should consider this person as musically talented. Someone who thinks a talent ought to be something that is solely metaphysical, defined in terms of one's dispositional qualities, would claim that the person in this world is indeed musically talented.

However, we would only be able to judge this person as musically talented if we were able to judge that her dispositional qualities, and the way she manifests them, are of an exceptionally high level; a talent after all denotes not just any

---

[11] Defining a talent as a disposition that is necessarily manifested in some way means that my account is not subject to the worry that dispositions are exhaustibly characterised in terms of their manifestation conditions, yet may never actually be manifested. In this way, we would worry that what we thought was a disposition would have to in fact be something else that is not defined solely in terms of how it is manifested, like a 'power', or an arrangement of structural properties (see Handfield 2010). My account gets around this worry, however, because talents are defined in terms of how they are manifested but also claims that those dispositions are necessarily manifested.

level of ability, but a high level of ability. It is only possible to compare someone's level of potential for a skill if we are able to make comparative judgements as to the level of her performance compared to others. In the case of the one-person world, we would only be able to label the musician as talented because we have someone or something to compare her to – we would have to refer to the existing comparison class of the talents of people we have experienced in our own world.

Within the one-person world itself, there is no comparison class, and there is no way to judge the comparative level of the person's musical potential. We may be able to judge that her musical potential allows her to express her ability in some way that is enjoyable or compelling; we might even be able to make an aesthetic judgement that the sounds she makes with her musical instruments are pleasing. We are not, however, able to make the necessary comparisons to judge whether her musical potential is expressed as a talent. This is both for epistemic and metaphysical reasons; not only are we epistemologically unable to make comparisons or judge the level of the person's skill acquisition, but there is no fact of the matter whether or not she is musically talented, because there are no other people that she could be compared with. Take the analogy of height: even if the person in the one-person world is tall by *our* standards, she is by herself unable to make any comparative judgements regarding her height because there is no comparison class. That is, there is no truth of the matter regarding her level of talent or height, because there is no such distinction of degree.

Second, it could also be objected that by understanding talent as determined by relative evaluative judgements about where certain comparative thresholds lie, I am conflating the metaphysical properties of what a talent is with what talents are merely *considered* to be. This might be a problem, for example, in a society that deems intelligence as belonging only to men, due to the fact that women are not valued enough to be classed as 'intelligent'. If a society sets its threshold for what counts as a talent in an arbitrary way like this, it will mean that whether or not someone is talented depends on that arbitrary threshold, irrespective of whether they actually *do* express high levels of potential. The problem is, therefore, that what counts as a talent is too epistemologically relative, and underplays the metaphysical facts about what counts as a talent.

It might be that we disagree about the right way to prescribe the evaluative judgements attached to the comparative levels of potential and skill acquisition. We may want to, and feel it is right for example, to condemn societies that prescribe different values to women as they do men, and consequently judge that the evaluative judgements underpinning their definition of what counts as a talent are mistaken. Nevertheless, even though there may be potential for normative disagreement and the fact that some societies might be mistaken regarding the calculation of their thresholds, this does not mean that talents are not comparative judgements and that these judgements are not socially relative. The fact that some societies' comparative thresholds may be morally inappropriate or wrong just means that we need to be careful about how we determine where the relevant thresholds should lie, and be able to give justifiable reasons for reaching our judgements. As such, it is perfectly permissible, on the account that I have been sketching, that we can retrospectively assess someone as talented in light of new information or more sophisticated value judgements. Nevertheless, it is still the case that talent is not merely a metaphysical phenomenon, describing only dispositional qualities in an individual, but is also an epistemological phenomenon that relies on comparative evaluative judgements that are socially relative regarding the way in which one's dispositional qualities are expressed.

1.6. Conclusion

In this chapter I have presented an account of talent understood as a high level of potential that is manifested and expressed in the excellent acquisition of a particular skill, demonstrated by the ease and speed with which that skill is acquired. In Section Two I made the case for understanding potential as a dispositional quality, and in Section Three I argued against the environmentalist position put forward by Howe *et al.*, which rejects the notion of natural potential being a causal factor in one's development. In Section Four, I argued that potential need not be understood purely as 'natural', but as resulting from a dynamic interaction between one's genetic code and one's environment. In Section Five, I argued that talents are not just high levels of potential, but one's potential as it is manifested and expressed in an above-average or excellent level of skill acquisition. This means that a talent is the expression of one's high level of potential, not merely the potential itself. I also argued that a definition of talent depends on evaluative judgements regarding the value of the skill itself and the various thresholds of comparison classes.

At the beginning of this chapter, I highlighted the terminological ambiguity surrounding the concept of a talent, both in the philosophical literature and in its everyday usage. This ambiguity seemed to conflate someone's potential for being excellent at a particular skill, with an already developed excellence in that skill. My sketch of the nature of talents has aimed to make sense of and incorporate both of these seemingly distinct notions of what a talents is. On the one hand, my account of talent acknowledges that a talent is a dispositional quality, a high level of potential for excellent skill acquisition. On the other hand, the account also acknowledges that if this potential is to be regarded as a talent, it has to be expressed or manifested in the excellent development of a particular skill. This explains why in everyday language we confuse a talent as being potential for excellence *and* an excellence – it is only once one's potential has been manifested in an excellent display of skill acquisition that it becomes a 'talent'.

As well as making sense of this apparent terminological confusion, my account of talent helps to make sense of three of the ways in which we value the development of our talents. First, by claiming that talents are the expression of a high level of potential for a particular skill, our talents are indexed to particular skills. In order for a talented person to develop a particular skill, her environment has to have within it the possibility for her to express and develop that skill; in other words, the opportunity to develop the skill has to be *on offer* in one's society. The skills that are on offer in society are ones that are valuable in some way. As a result, we value the development of talents in part because the skills they enable us to acquire are themselves valuable.

There may be many reasons why a particular skill is valued by one's society; we might appeal to the skill's instrumental value or claim that it is valuable for its own sake. We may even disagree about the type and level of value afforded to certain skills by others and different societies; these value judgements will most likely be made on a case by case basis, depending on the context in which one's talents are being developed. It may be the case, however, that a particular skill is considered to be *immoral* or has a negative value attached to it in a particular society. For example, we might often refer to someone's talent to upset people around her, or a talent for manipulating others, and these are not skills that we automatically or intuitively consider to be positively valued. In these cases it might seem that it is not the case that a talent must be valued in the way I have been arguing throughout this chapter. If these skills really are to be classed as talents, then it is important to note that even if a skill is not positively valued in some parts of society or in one particular culture, it may be valued in others. The skill of manipulating others (if this is to be classed as a talent as opposed to something that a person is merely *good at*) may have beneficial instrumental value in some cases, for example, when trying to win a political election. In this way, irrespective of how the value judgements are made, and whether or not we deem them to be plausible judgements to make, it is still the case that talents are valued in part due to the particular skill that is being developed and the way in which that skill is valued in itself.

Second, we also value talents because of the way in which they are comparatively assessed. In this chapter I claimed that what counts as a talent is dependent on comparison thresholds, and these thresholds are usually set to pick out only a limited number of people who are considered to be 'excellent' (insofar as their level of skill is above a comparative threshold). As a result, we value talents because they pick out people with a *rare* ability for acquiring a particular skill. Because talents are rare, this means that they are in short supply, and we value resources that are in short supply because we have to look after the amount that we do have for fear of them being exhausted. We cherish talents because they pick out an excellence that is uncommon, and when we fail to develop our talents we are consequently wasting something that is rare and in short supply.

Third, the fact that a talent is a dispositional quality indexed to a particular person means that it is *unique* – it manifests differently in each person according to the various dispositional qualities of that person and the environment in which she finds herself. And so, when a person fails to develop their talent we may think that something of value has been wasted; a person's talent cannot be exchanged, and it belongs uniquely to them. If the talent is not developed then this value of individuality may be lost (see for example Mill: 39-68; Cottingham: 72).

The account of talent that I have argued for in this chapter has elucidated three of the reasons why we place value on talents and their development: talents are rare, they are unique, and they are indexed to skill domains that are valued in some way by society. In the proceeding chapters, I examine whether the value that we place on talents and their development gives rise to the claim that one has good prudential reasons or a moral obligation develop one's talents. I continue this task in the next chapter by critically assessing whether Kant's claim that we have a moral duty to develop our talents.

Chapter Two

The Kantian Duty to Develop One's Talents

2.1. Introduction

We often express disappointment or regret when we hear of cases in which talents have been wasted or neglected. This common negative reaction can be explained, in part, by the assumption that developing one's talents is valuable in some way for those who are talented, or for others around them. For instance, we might think that the artist Paul Gauguin made the right choice by leaving his family and moving to Paris in order to develop and make a success of his talent for painting; if instead he stayed at home with his family, then we might have judged that he did something wrong. We make these evaluative judgements because we consider the development of Gauguin's talent to be valuable for himself, and perhaps also valuable for those around him and society at large. In order to understand this value more fully, we can ask what grounds these evaluative judgements when it comes to talents and their development: what constitutes the apparent wrongness of Gauguin, or any other talented person, failing to develop their talents?

One answer to this question is to understand the person who fails to develop her talents as doing something *morally* wrong. This wrongness could be grounded in straightforward consequentialist reasons. For example, developing one's talent may result in the maximisation of beneficial consequences for society, with the talented person becoming a more productive and efficient producer of resources, and so contributing to the more productive and efficient organisation of society. Failing to develop one's talents would withhold these positive effects from benefiting others in this way. In other words, the wrongness would be grounded in the failure to act in a way that maximises utility.

However, the consequentialist account does not capture the only reasons we might want to give when we claim that failing to develop one's talents is morally wrong. We could also base our evaluative judgement on the fact that the talented person herself has done something wrong, irrespective of whether utility is maximised. Kant, for example, explicitly claims that we have an imperfect, positive moral duty to ourselves to develop our talents. This duty is not grounded in virtue of what we owe to others or what will produce the best consequences, but in the respect that we owe to ourselves as moral agents. According to Kant, a rational moral agent could not will the neglect of her talents without violating the Categorical Imperative, and as such, failing to develop one's talents is immoral.

In this chapter, I will analyse the two arguments in support of Kant's claim that we have a moral duty to develop our talents, and demonstrate why both of these are unsuccessful. The first of Kant's arguments appeals to his Formula of Universal Law, which provides justification for the claim that the duty to develop one's talents is an 'imperfect' duty; I discuss this argument in Section Two. In Section Three I discuss Kant's second argument, which appeals to the Formula of Humanity, offering an explanation for why the duty ought to be considered specifically as one that we owe to ourselves rather than to others.

Kant's arguments are subject to three objections, and in Section Four I deal with each in turn. The first objection deals with Kant's distinction between imperfect and perfect duties. I argue that if there is a moral duty to develop one's talents, then it is not necessarily imperfect as Kant claims, but also has the potential to be a perfect duty. Second, it could be objected that the duty is not one that is owed to oneself, but instead must always be other-directed. In response to this, I argue that Kant can overcome this objection, and that the moral duty to develop one's talents can plausibly be understood in Kantian terms as a duty that is owed to oneself rather than to others. Finally, I argue that if Kant is to succeed in claiming that one has a moral duty to develop one's talents, then he needs to be able to explain why developing talents is morally superior to developing any other competencies that one may have. I conclude that Kant cannot successfully argue for this moral superiority of talents over competencies, and as a result, Kant cannot successfully derive a moral duty to develop one's talents from the Categorical Imperative. He may be able to justify a wider duty of self-development or self-perfection, but if there is such a duty, it does not necessarily include as part of it a requirement to develop one's talents. As such, if there is a moral obligation to develop one's talents, it cannot be a Kantian one.[12]

Before I begin discussing Kant's Formula of Universal Law in Section Two, it is important to note two things. First, Kant understands a talent as a "natural gift" and "excellence", which is constituted by "the subject's natural predisposition" (Anthropology: 115). This emphasis on talent as distinctly 'natural' seems to contrast with the account of talents I proposed in Chapter One, which claims that the dispositional qualities of a talent are not natural, but emerge from a dynamic interaction between genetic and environmental stimuli. However, as I will demonstrate in Section Four of this chapter, Kant's understanding of the nature of talents is compatible with the account I offer in Chapter One, understood as an advantageous level of potential that is manifested in the excellent acquisition of a particular skill.

Second, the success of Kant's claims regarding talent development rest on his underlying deontological account of morality, which emphasises the value of intentions and motivations behind an action, rather than the potential or actual consequences of that action. For Kant, moral worth comes from having a good will that acts only from duty to the moral law, acting in such a way merely because it is one's duty to do so.[13] For morality to be normatively binding on us all, Kant claims that the moral law must consist of categorical imperatives rather than hypothetical ones, so that morality is objective and unconditional, without reference to any other contingent end or subjective desires. Kant considers the moral law to be constituted by only one Categorical Imperative that can be iterated by different formulations. It is when elucidating and exemplifying these formulations that Kant considers the development of one's talents to be a moral

---

[12] Even though I argue that Kant cannot plausibly claim we have a moral duty to develop our talents, it might be the case that we have other moral reasons for developing our talents, and that failing to do so is morally wrong, and so morally required, for those reasons. For example, in the next chapter I entertain the reasons given by the theory of Moral Perfectionism, and I have already mentioned briefly the reasons that could be given by consequentialism.

[13] Note that there is a distinction between a person lacking moral worth due to their actions not being generated from adherence to the moral law, and an action being morally wrong because it contradicts a duty generated from the moral law. See Derek Parfit on this point (Parfit 2011: 275-300), and thanks to Campbell Brown for highlighting this.

duty, insofar as failure to do so would contradict and violate the Categorical Imperative.

For the purposes of this chapter, I will assume that Kant's account of morality is plausible, such that morality is grounded in the duties that are generated from the Categorical Imperative and that moral worth is derived from acting in accordance with these duties. Given this concession, my claim is that *even if* we accept Kant's account of morality, we can still object to the way that he characterises and grounds the potential duty that one may have to develop one's talents. Although the focus of this chapter is directed specifically towards the Kantian duty to develop one's talents, analysing this duty also has implications for how we ought to interpret Kant's overall moral project, questioning the ambiguous nature of his distinction between imperfect and perfect duties, and the plausibility of moral duties that are owed to oneself.

2.2. The Formula of Universal Law

In the *Groundwork for the Metaphysics of Morals*, Kant initially claims that we have a moral duty to develop our talents when he articulates the first formulation of the Categorical Imperative, the Formula of Universal Law: "act only in accordance with the maxim through which you can at the same time will that it become a universal law" (GW 4:421).[14] A maxim is explained by Kant as a "subjective principle of volition", which specifies the reason for which a particular agent has acted or acts in a particular circumstance (GW 4:401). And so, according to the Formula of Universal Law, an action is morally permissible only if one can will that the maxim by which one is acting can be universalised, such that anyone

---

[14] Kant goes on to reiterate this formula as the imperative to "act as if the maxim of your action were to become by your will a universal law of *nature*" (GW 4:421, emphasis added). Although in this second iteration the universal law is one of 'nature', the difference is subtle and does not substantially alter the plausibility of the arguments that will be offered in this chapter. As a result, I take both iterations of the first formula of the Categorical Imperative to be equivalent in meaning. Christine Korsgaard, for example, does the same (Korsgaard 1983).

else can, without contradiction, will and act on the basis of that same maxim in the same circumstances.

There are two ways in which this universalisation test could fail. First of all, when universalising one's specific maxim for an action, an inconsistency could occur at the level of 'conception', which occurs if the "maxim cannot even be thought without contradiction" (GW 4:424). Kant gives the example of making a false promise, deliberately making a promise to someone without the intention of keeping it. When running that particular maxim through the universalisation test, it becomes apparent, so Kant claims, that if everyone were to will the same maxim then the institution of promising would break down. This is because promising depends on trusting that those who make promises do actually intend to keep them; if no-one intended to keep their promises then this assumption of trust would be lost. Consequently, it is impossible to simultaneously will the maxim to make a false promise, and also will that it be universalised without an inherent contradiction; that is, we cannot conceive of a world in which everyone (successfully) acts on the maxim to make a false promise. Kant therefore concludes that we have a moral duty not to make false promises, because making false promises would violate the Categorical Imperative.

The duty that results from violating the Formula of Universal Law in this way, with a contradiction in conception, is what Kant classifies as a *perfect* duty. This type of duty is a "strict or narrower (unremitting) duty" (GW 4:424) and "admits no exception in favour of inclination" (GW 4:421fn). A perfect duty specifically forbids a particular maxim, with no room for interpretation or choice from the agent herself as to the way in which, and the extent to which, the duty must be followed.

However, failing to develop one's talents does not violate the Categorical Imperative in the same way that making a false promise does: it does not amount to a contradiction in conception. There is no inconsistency in conceiving of a world in which we all (successfully) act upon the maxim to neglect our talents; it might not be a particularly productive or exciting world, but nevertheless, such a world could be consistently imagined. Instead, the duty to develop one's talents occurs as a result of a contradiction in *willing*, which is the second way in which the universalisation test could fail. Kant explains how the maxim of neglecting one's talents contradicts the Formula of Universal Law as follows:

> A [person] finds in himself a talent that by means of some cultivation could make him a human being useful for all sorts of purposes. However, he finds himself in comfortable circumstances and prefers to give himself up to pleasure than to trouble himself with enlarging and improving his fortunate natural predispositions. But he still asks himself whether his maxim of neglecting his natural gifts, besides being consistent with his propensity to amusement, is also consistent with what one calls duty. He now sees that a nature could indeed always subsist with such a universal law, although […] the human being should let his talents rust and be concerned with devoting his life merely to idleness, amusement, procreation – in a word, to enjoyment; only he cannot possibly *will* that this become a universal law or be put in us as such by means of natural instinct. For, as a rational being he necessarily wills that all the capacities in him be developed, since they serve him and are given to him for all sorts of possible purposes (GW 4:423).

In this passage, Kant suggests that if the maxim of neglecting to develop one's talents was universalised and acted upon, then we would find ourselves in a world in which no talents are developed at all. Willing such a maxim, however, would be irrational because the cultivation of talents is necessary for achieving all sorts of ends that are useful for a person, and for society to function efficiently and productively (O'Neill: 123-5). In order to rationally will that I neglect the development of my own talents, I would have to rely on others sufficiently developing their talents to provide the goods that are necessary and valuable for a decent life. This, Kant argues, results in a contradiction: due to the universalisation of my maxim to neglect my talents, I would have to will at the same time that others develop their talents to provide me with the goods I need, and also will that no talents are to be developed at all. Such a contradiction violates the Formula of Universal Law, and as such, Kant concludes that we have a duty not to neglect the development of our talents.

The duty that results from violating the Categorical Imperative in this way, through a contradiction in willing, is what Kant calls an *imperfect* duty. Unlike a perfect duty, this type of duty allows for some degree of inclination and choice in how, and the extent to which, the duty is to be fulfilled by a particular agent (GW 4:424). As such, an imperfect duty is indeterminate, specifying only the *end* that ought to be brought about, rather than stipulating the limitations and constraints on how we are allowed to bring about that end and fulfil our duty. Kant claims that because the duty to develop one's talents is imperfect, this means that "no rational principle prescribes specifically how far one should go in cultivating one's capacities [...] the different situations in which a human being may find themselves make a man's choice of the occupation for which he should cultivate his talents very much a matter for him to decide as he chooses" (MM 6:391-3). This means that the Formula of Universal Law merely tells us that we must not neglect talents that could be cultivated for the good of ourselves and society. It does not tell us, however, how best to achieve this requirement by indicating, for example, which talents we should develop and to what extent; such a decision is up to the agent herself.

Initially it seems as if Kant characterises the imperfect duty one has to develop one's talents as relying on the beneficial consequences that one can achieve for oneself and society; in the passage above he writes that cultivating one's talents could make one "useful for all sorts of purposes" (see again GW 4:423). It could be the case that the only reason one would want to develop one's talent is because of the valuable consequences that may arise from doing so. However, for Kant, appealing to the beneficial consequences of an action does not in turn justify why that action is a moral duty. Even though imperfect duties only specify ends rather than particular actions, this does not mean that the duty is contingent on the advantageous consequences that may arise from acting in accordance with that duty. What grounds the moral unworthiness of failing to develop one's talents is not the useful purposes that we would be missing out on, or the fact that society might fail to flourish. Rather, the duty is grounded in the rational inconsistency that arises when universalising one's maxim results in a contradiction in willing, and thus violates the Formula of Universal Law (MM 6:391; see also Paton 1971: 155; Sedgwick 2008: 120; Timmerman 2007: 97).[15]

---

[15] Initially it seems as if there may be examples of 'talent-neglecting' maxims that could be morally permissible for Kant, for instance, the maxim that I neglect my talents in order to raise my children who are dependent upon me. This seems permissible, presumably because the reason for neglecting talents in this instance is the fostering and respect of my duty to my children, and this is an instantiation of the duty to respect humanity (which

It could initially be objected against Kant's account that if *everyone* willed and acted upon the maxim to develop their talents, then this would also result in an inconsistency of willing and thus violate the Formula of Universal Law. This would mean that people's skills were so far developed that they consequently had no desire to fulfil the menial everyday tasks that are necessary for the efficient running of society. The optimal situation might be one in which only some people develop their talents, and as a result, the maxim to neglect one's talents would not result in a problematic contradiction in willing, as Kant claims.

However, this objection is not successful. It fails to recognise that abilities come in different shapes and sizes, based on the dispositional qualities of each individual and the way that these qualities are expressed through various skills. As such, given that each person will have different levels of potential for a particular skill, some peoples' levels of ability will be suited to and appropriate for the everyday menial tasks that are referred to in the objection as necessary for the efficient running of society. In which case, it would not be irrational for everyone to develop their talents, as different levels of ability in society would cover the whole spectrum of necessary skills needed for society to function.[16] This means that it could still plausibly be the case that a contradiction in willing arises when I universalise my maxim to neglect the development of my talents.[17]

I will go on to discuss in Section 2.4.3). However, passing this maxim through the universalisation test would still arise in a contradiction in willing; if everyone acted according to such a maxim, or a maxim that neglected talent development in favour of other duties, then hardly any talents would be developed. This results in a contradiction because I would at the same time be willing that others develop their talents to provide me with the goods that I need, but also that talents should not be developed when they conflict with other duties. Importantly, this issue points to a wider problem with Kant's account of morality: it is unclear what we should do when duties conflict, especially considering that different iterations of the Categorical Imperative may specify different duties. The fact that one may neglect one's talents for other morally permissible reasons does not by itself negate Kant's justification for the duty to develop one's talents. Thanks to Robert Cowan for his comments on this point.

[16] It could be argued that these more modest or 'menial' abilities would not be considered as talents, at least on the account of talents that I propose in Chapter One. I will deal with this point later in the present chapter, specifically in Section 4.3.

[17] This does not mean to say that the Kantian moral duty to develop one's talents is dependent upon or grounded on contingent facts about the level of each person's disposition for acquiring particular skills. Instead, the moral requirement is grounded in

In Section Four I will discuss further objections to Kant's justification that we have a duty to develop one's talents as it arises from the Formula of Universal Law, specifically with regards to whether the duty is plausibly to be considered as *imperfect* rather than *perfect*. Before doing so, however, in the next section I discuss Kant's second argument, arising from his explanation of the second iteration of the Categorical Imperative, the Formula of Humanity.

2.3. The Formula of Humanity

The Formula of Humanity states that one must "act in such a way that you always treat humanity, whether in your own person or in the person of any other, never simply as a means, but always at the same time as an end", and as such, one's maxim should always be "consistent with the idea of humanity *as an end in itself*" (GW 4:429). According to Kant, it is our rationality that characterises human nature, and our rational nature ought to be valued as an end in itself, as unconditionally valuable. Kant characterises this rational nature as the ability to set ends and "rule over" ourselves, bringing all our "capacities and inclination under [our] control" (MM 6:408; see also Paton 1971: 151). As such, to treat an agent as an end rather than a mere means amounts to respecting and valuing her humanity, which is for Kant to respect and value her rational nature – the capacity to set ends for herself and adopt the means to produce those ends.

For example, making false promises is not only immoral for Kant because it violates the Formula of Universal Law through a contradiction in conception, but also because it violates the Formula of Humanity. This violation occurs because making a false promise results in making use of another person merely for one's own gain; instead, we need to recognise and respect the other person as someone with the unconditionally valuable capacity for rationality, as someone who is able

---

our rational nature, but given that the duty is imperfect, the way in which each agent fulfils this requirement is subject to an element of latitude and choice. One consideration that could play a role in how an agent chooses to fulfil her duty may be based on her levels of potential for acquiring particular skills. These contingent facts merely *inform* an agent when deciding how to fulfil her duty, and do not *ground* the duty itself.

to will and act upon the ends that she sets for herself. Breaking our promise to that person is a sign of disrespect for her rational capacities, due to the fact that we are treating her in a way that she would not consent to, and as such, disrespecting her capacity to 'rule over' herself, by setting ends and adopting the means for those ends.

According to Kant, however, we do not only have a duty to respect the humanity in others; we also have a duty to recognise and respect the humanity in ourselves. Kant claims that the duty to develop one's talents is such a duty that one owes to oneself rather than to others, because neglecting one's talents amounts to neglecting and disrespecting one's own rational nature. The duty that one has to develop one's talents as grounded in the Formula of Humanity is explained by Kant as follows:

> A human being has a duty to himself to cultivate his natural powers (powers of spirit, mind, and body), as means to all sorts of possible ends. He owes it to himself (as a rational being) not to leave idle and, as it were, rusting away the natural predispositions and capacities that his reason can someday use [...] as a being capable of ends (of making objects his ends), he must owe the use of his powers not merely to natural instinct but rather to the freedom by which he determines their scope. Hence the basis on which he should develop his capacities (for all sorts of ends) is not regard for the advantages that their cultivation can provide; for the advantage might [...] turn out on the side of his crude natural needs. Instead, it is a command of morally practical reason and a *duty* of a human being to himself to cultivate his capacities (some among them more than others, insofar as people have different ends), and to be in a pragmatic respect a human being equal to the end of his existence (MM 6:444-5).

As with the example of talent development explained in the Formula of Universal Law, Kant could be interpreted as relying on teleological and prudential justification for claiming that we ought to develop our capacities. He claims in the passage just cited that we owe it to ourselves to nurture our capacities because they are 'useful' to us, as a means to all sorts of 'possible ends'. In another passage Kant further suggests this teleological interpretation: he claims that "a human being has a duty to himself to be a useful member of the world" (MM 6:445).

However, it is not the usefulness or consequences of developing one's talents that grounds this moral duty. Rather, being a worthy and useful member of society just is to respect humanity's rational nature as an end in itself, and amounts to a moral agent respecting "the worth of humanity in his own person, which he ought not to degrade" (MM 6:445; see also Denis: 330). It is because developing one's talents is in the service of this rational capacity that it is not merely valued because of some contingent end or advantage. Kant claims that talents should be developed because they promote the excellent development of capacities that can be used in the service of one's rationality. We therefore have a moral duty to develop our talents insofar as failing to do so means that we fail to respect and promote the value of our own rational capacities. As such, the duty to develop one's talents is part of the duty to develop our capacities more generally; to perfect them fully and nurture their development as part of the respect for our humanity. Practical reason works through the development of our capacities, enabling us to set ends and adopt the means to achieve those ends. By developing our talents, we are working to develop our capacities, or at least a certain sub-set of those capacities.

Kant distinguishes the duty to respect one's own humanity (rationality) as having a negative and positive aspect. The negative aspect states the command to *preserve* one's rational nature, to "live in conformity with nature", whilst the positive aspect states the command to *perfect* and *further* one's rational nature, to "make yourself more perfect than mere nature has made you" (MM 6:419). This positive demand for self-perfection is grounded in the understanding that our rational natures have an inclination towards excellence – "furtherance" and "greater perfection" (GW 4:430). Failing to act on the duty to develop one's talents means that one would neglect and fail to further one's own worth as a rational, moral agent. Again, it is important to note that it is respect for one's rationality, as generated by the Categorical Imperative, that grounds this duty for self-perfection, and not the consequential positive benefits of prudential flourishing that may emerge from fulfilling the duty. The duty itself is not conditional or instrumental, but generated from the unconditional Categorical Imperative as a duty for self-perfection, and so necessarily including the development of one's talents which is according to Kant considered to be the epitome of perfect and excellent capacity development.

Even though the duty of self-perfection is generated from the respect one ought to give one's rational capacities, developing one's talents need not be limited to those talents that are indexed to skills that only promote one's rational powers or intellect. Kant considers the development of all kinds of talents to be necessary for the perfection of one's humanity; he claims that perfecting humanity involves cultivating "your powers of mind *and* body so that they are fit to realize any ends you might encounter", and that we ought to develop "any capacities whatever for furthering ends set forth by reason" (MM 6:391-3, emphasis added). This means that perfecting one's rationality also involves the nurturing of one's intellectual *and* physical capacities (Denis: 327). Developing one's talents, therefore, gives an agent the ability to set all kinds of ends (not just intellectual ends) and provide oneself with the means to attain these ends. Failing to develop one's talents would result in the prevention of one's own ability to pursue the means to the ends that one sets for oneself. As such, the duty that we have to ourselves to develop our talents is a positive, imperfect duty, that rests on the justification that self-perfection is necessary for treating one's humanity as an end in itself.

Furthermore, for Kant, the duty of self-perfection has to be understood specifically as a moral requirement, and not a prudential one. This is because, for Kant, moral worth is grounded in acting from duty to the Categorical Imperative; this can only be achieved through the exercising of one's rational capacities, so that one can autonomously bind oneself to and formulate maxims that are accountable to the different formulations of the Categorical Imperative. As such, it is one's rational nature that makes one's moral agency possible. As Nelson Potter claims, for Kant "[a]ll duties to oneself have to do with the self as a moral agent, and as a self having the ability to impose duties on itself, that is, with maintaining and developing the self's specifically moral capacities" (Potter 2002: 375). Because failing to develop one's talents is to neglect and disvalue one's ability to set and act upon ends for oneself, for Kant this is necessarily a *moral* failing, as neglecting one's rationality is to neglect the capacity that enables one to participate as a moral agent, insofar as you are neglecting in an important way the development, preservation and expression of practical reason. In this way, the duty that one has to oneself to develop one's talents has to be understood as part of the duty to enable oneself to respect and perfect one's moral capacity to act in accordance with duty (Potter 1998: 44).

Given that the duty to develop one's talents is a duty that one owes to oneself, this makes the duty central to Kant's overall moral project. Not only are duties to oneself moral duties because they express the requirement to value and perfect one's moral agency, but according to Kant, they take priority over all other types of moral duties; he claims that without duties to oneself there "would be no [moral] duties whatsoever" (MM 6:417). This is because as a moral agent I "recognize that I am under obligation to others only insofar as I at the same time put myself under obligation, since by the law by virtue of which I regard myself as being under obligation proceeds in every case from my practical reason; and in being constrained by my own reasons, I am also the one constraining myself" (MM 6:417). Being able to act in accordance with the moral law thus requires an agent to express and utilise one's practical rationality, and as such, the duty that one has to oneself to respect and perfect one's rational capacities is necessary to make this kind of moral action possible.

By claiming that duties to oneself take priority over duties to others, Kant is making a transcendental claim, that duties to oneself are the condition of possibility for duties to others. This is because, according to Kant, the moral law is necessarily one that we give to ourselves through the formulation of maxims in accordance with the Categorical Imperative. More specifically, it is due to one's own acceptance that the moral law is grounded in one's own rationality and volitional consistency that one understands oneself as bound to that law: *I* am the one that recognises the binding nature of the Categorical Imperative, and *I* am the one that formulates maxims for myself, judging that they are consistent with the moral law. Consequently, my moral action is constrained and limited by my own reason, which means that without attending to, realising and perfecting my capacity for reason, I cannot act as a moral agent in the first place. Duties to oneself are therefore fundamental to morality as providing morality's condition of possibility, and as a result, their priority is transcendental; duties to oneself *make possible* our rational and moral agency.[18]

It would be a mistake, however, to interpret Kant's transcendental claim regarding the priority of duties to oneself as also being a 'formal' claim, asserting that just because duties to oneself are self-legislated then they are necessarily owed to that same legislating self. This would mean that *all* duties are duties to oneself, in virtue of the fact that Kant considers all duties to be grounded in one's own practical rationality. Timmerman suggests that Kant may have this formal argument in mind (Timmerman 2007: 88), and Potter too, claiming that "all duties are partially [duties to oneself] because the agent must use the powers of self-constraint that are presupposed by any duty to recognize and undertake any duty at all" (Potter 2002: 376).

However, as Andrews Reath has argued, interpreting Kant in this way confuses the legislator of the duty (the one who determines *that* I have a duty), with the person to whom the duty is owed. Just because each of us is our own moral legislators, this does not mean that *all* of our moral obligations are owed to ourselves. The person to whom one has the duty is not always in the legislative position but is the "individual whose condition, interests, circumstance, or relationship or past dealing with oneself, and so on, give reasons for action that make a special claim on one's conduct" (Reath: 361). This means that the person to whom one's moral duty is owed provides one with the reasons for why one is obligated to act in a particular way, in accordance with the moral law, and irrespective of who legislates over the formulation of the relevant maxim (ibid., 362).

Even though duties owed to oneself are grounded in the recognition that it is one's own self that makes a claim on one's moral activity, this does not mean that the priority of duties to oneself arises as a result of the formal autonomous

---

[18] Paton also seems to make such a claim, albeit implicitly, about the priority of the moral duties we owe to ourselves as being transcendental in this way. He writes that "in some sense [duties to oneself] are to be regarded as having greater importance in our endeavour to make sense of morality", because they lay "the very foundations of morality by realizing a value without which morality could not exist" (Paton 1971: 229).

nature of moral legislation (ibid., 367). Instead, the fundamentality of duties to oneself arises due to the fact that the preservation and perfection of one's own rational nature is a precondition for the binding nature of morality. Duties to oneself consequently take priority over duties to others because they provide the condition of possibility for all and any moral duty to be generated in the first place, through a moral agent's preservation and perfection of her rational nature.

The Formula of Humanity therefore initially seems to provide Kant with the justification for the moral duty to develop one's talents as being one that we owe to ourselves: respect for our own humanity requires that we preserve and perfect our rational capacities. As a result, failing to develop one's talents would be to act contrary to the Formula of Humanity, in that one would fail to respect and promote the development of the capacities that can be used in the service of one's practical rationality. Not only would this violate the respect that one ought to have for one's own human nature, but due to the fact that duties to oneself are the condition of possibility for all other duties, it would also undermine the possibility of morality altogether.[19]

2.4. Objections

Having outlined the arguments that Kant gives for his claim that there is a positive, imperfect duty to oneself to develop one's talents, I will now turn to three objections that can be levelled against his account. First, I argue that if there is a duty to develop one's talents, then it is not necessarily imperfect as Kant claims, but also has the potential to be a perfect duty. This re-classification of the duty, however, does not negate the more substantial claim that there is a moral duty to develop one's talents, but merely highlights that the duty could in some

---

[19] Undermining the possibility of morality in this way is only a problem if one is a Kantian about morality and believes that moral worth necessarily stems from our worth as rational agents. If, on the other hand, rationality is not the ground of moral worth, then failing to respect or perfect practical rationality is not a problem intrinsic to the nature of morality. In other words, morality could still be possible if we neglect our rational natures, but we might deem, for other moral reasons, that developing our rationality is morally beneficial (such as, for example, the value of the relevant consequences).

circumstances be a 'narrow' one that does not allow any interpretation or choice from the agent as to how, and the extent to which, the duty must be fulfilled. Second, I will discuss the objection that the duty is not one that is necessarily owed to oneself, but is instead a duty that one owes to others. I argue that Kant can overcome this objection, and the duty to develop one's talents should indeed be one that is owed to oneself. Finally, I object to Kant's argument by demonstrating that he cannot generate the moral priority of developing specifically one's talents, rather than any other capacities or non-talent abilities that one may have. I argue that this objection successfully undermines Kant's justification for the moral duty to develop one's talents.

2.4.1. Imperfect and Perfect Duties

Kant claims that the duty to develop one's talents is imperfect; the duty arises from a contradiction in willing when it is tested against the Formula of Universal Law, and as such, allows for some latitude in how to fulfil the action that is demanded by the duty. If the difference between perfect and imperfect duties was explained by Kant simply as the difference between violating the Categorical Imperative through either a contradiction in conception or willing, then the distinction would simply be a term of art. However, Kant goes on to claim that perfect and imperfect duties are differently characterised with regards to how much latitude an agent has at her discretion to choose how she goes about fulfilling her duty. On the one hand, perfect duties are 'strict' and 'narrow', allowing no latitude for the agent's own inclination as to how best to fulfil the duty. On the other hand, imperfect duties are 'wide' and 'latitudinous', allowing for an agent's judgement and inclination when fulfilling the duty.

It has been objected that Kant's distinction between perfect and imperfect duties is implausible; it seems as if both perfect *and* imperfect duties can be fulfilled with a certain amount of an agent's free choice and latitude. For example, when I promise to pay my friend the £500 that I owe her, I consequently have a duty to keep that promise. According to the Formula of Universal Law, this duty is perfect and as such does not allow any latitude in how the duty should be fulfilled. However, this is not the case. I can go about keeping that promise, and thus fulfilling my duty, in a number of different ways – paying my friend by cheque, in £10 notes, meeting her in person, sending the money by post, or handing the money over with my left or right hand. As a result, it is not clear that perfect duties really do specify a fully comprehensive was of implementing one's maxim.

Given the fact that even perfect duties can give rise to an agent's discretion, it is argued that the distinction between perfect and imperfect duties cannot be based on how much latitude the duty gives an agent. As Schroeder claims, "*all* duties turn out to be imperfect" because "virtually all duties will be infinitely disjunctive" (Schroeder: 7, referencing Stocker 1967). It even seems as if Kant too considers all duties derived from the Categorical Imperative to be partly imperfect, allowing for some latitude of choice; he claims that "if the [moral law] can prescribe only the maxim of actions, not actions themselves, this is a sign that it leaves a playroom for free choice in following (complying with) the law, that is, that the law cannot specify precisely in what way one is to act and how much one is to do by the action for an end that is also a duty" (MM 6:390).

If it were the case that all duties are actually imperfect, allowing an agent latitude of choice with regards to how to fulfil her duty, this would mean there is no substantial reason for Kant to classify duties as either imperfect or perfect. As a result, the way in which an agent fulfils her imperfect duty to develop her talents and the perfect duty to keep her promise would no longer be considered as allowing different levels of an agent's discretion. However, there are ways in which we could attempt to specify a substantial distinction between perfect and imperfect duties on Kant's behalf. I will reject three of these attempts and finally argue that the distinction between the two types of duties should be one of degree and not kind.

First, we could argue that perfect duties are specified negatively, whilst imperfect duties are positive; the perfect duty to refrain from making a false promise is explained in terms of the fact that we are *not* allowed to make a false promise, whilst the duty to develop one's talents is explained in terms of the fact that we *ought* to nurture our talents. However, this distinction does not hold, as both types of duties can be spelled out either negatively or positively. With regards to refraining from making false promises, one's perfect duty is just as much to *keep* one's promise as it is to *not* make a false one. With regards to developing talents, one's imperfect duty is just as much to *develop* one's talents as it is to *not neglect* their development.

Second, Rainbolt has suggested that the distinction might be explained in terms of the metaphysical difference between an 'act-type' and an 'act-token'. An act-type is a general or universal property that an action has, such as the generic action of 'drinking wine', 'writing a paper' or 'playing tennis'. An act-token, by contrast, is a particular action that instantiates a general act-type at any given moment. For example, the universal act-type of 'writing a paper' can be made into a particular act-token by taking into consideration how that act-type is instantiated (Rainbolt: 234-5). Rainbolt suggests that we could understand a perfect duty as one that specifies an agent's particular act-token, with an imperfect duty specifying only a general act-type (ibid., 239). Stocker suggests a similar distinction, claiming that perfect duties are meant to "individuate" the acts that an agent must carry out to fulfil the duty, whilst an imperfect duty only "characterises" those acts (Stocker: 510).

It is not clear, however, whether perfect duties really do specify individuated acts or act-tokens, rather than characteristic general act-types. The duty to refrain from suicide, for example, is a perfect duty according to Kant, but this duty does not necessarily specify an act-token that must be used to successfully instantiate the act-type of 'not committing suicide'. Furthermore, it seems as if the duty to develop one's talents could specify a particular act-token that instantiates the act-type of 'developing a talent', perhaps by considering who is developing their talent and under what particular circumstances. In this way, both perfect and imperfect duties can either be metaphysically underdetermined, such that they are considered to be act-types, or particularly determined, such that they are considered to be act-tokens (Stocker: 509). Therefore, the distinction doesn't hold, and both Rainbolt and Stocker ultimately reject this interpretation.

A third option to specify the distinction between perfect and imperfect duties is to highlight the difference in moral relevancy of the choice that is given to agents; a perfect duty does not allow latitude of choice with regards to morally relevant properties, whilst an imperfect duty does (Stocker: 509-512; Rainbolt:

245). For example, in some cultures it might be morally relevant to specify how I give the money I borrowed back to my friend – doing so with my left hand could be classified as offensive. In this way, the perfect duty would specify that I should not pay back the money I owe to my friend by using my left hand.

However, if this distinction was to hold, it would mean that an imperfect duty allows free choice with respect to morally relevant features of an action; this could potentially allow for morally impermissible consequences. For instance, even though the duty to develop one's talents is imperfect, it should not be the case that an agent is allowed to fulfil that duty in *any* way, by offending or harming people, or engaging in activities that are considered to be morally impermissible. As a result, it should be the case that even an imperfect duty, and not just a perfect one, will have to specify and constrain an agent's actions with regards to what is morally relevant or permissible.[20]

The three previous suggestions for specifying the difference between perfect and imperfect duties have distinguished ways in which the duties are different in *kind*. Conversely, I suggest that the difference is best thought of as one of *degree* or *scale*. Rainbolt argues along these lines, claiming that all duties have the potential to allow for an agent's discretion, by referring to five main categories: the time, place and manner in which the duty is fulfilled, the object that the duty is directed towards, and the number of act-tokens used to successfully fulfil the duty (Rainbolt: 234). A duty is completely perfect when it specifies exactly only one particular action with respect to all of these five categories, and a completely imperfect duty will give an agent free choice with

---

[20] Schroeder thinks that the way to solve the problem of the distinction between imperfect and perfect duties is to consider imperfect duties as duties held primarily by a group, with each individual assigned part of the obligation to discharge (Schroeder: 19). However, it is not certain that this distinction is any more clear-cut than the previous ones that I have already rejected in this section. Depending on how an agent formulates her maxim based on the particular circumstances, all her duties could be said to be held by a group, insofar as she is a member of a social community, with her actions indirectly and directly affecting others. Her duty to refrain from suicide, to refrain from making a false promise, or to develop her talents, could all be part of a larger duty that is held by a group, in place to secure the prosperity of society. Therefore, Schroeder's suggestion does not plausibly differentiate between the two types of duties, nor does it account for the ways in which latitude plays a part in fulfilling each obligation.

regards to how each of these categories is to be met. Most duties, however, will not be completely perfect or imperfect, but be somewhere in-between. Kant also seems to imply that the distinction should be thought of in these terms, claiming that "[t]he wider the duty, therefore, the more imperfect is a man's obligation to actions [...] the more leeway that a duty gives to how you could go about fulfilling it, the wider or imperfect that duty can be said to be" (MM 6:390; see also Schroeder: 3).

If the distinction between perfect and imperfect duties is one of degree, then each duty will be as narrow or particular as it needs to be in order to accurately specify what is required of an agent to successfully fulfil the duty. This means that the duty to develop one's talents is not necessarily imperfect as Kant claims, but rather the amount of choice an agent has when fulfilling the duty depends on the particular circumstances in which she finds herself. For example, the duty will be more particular if there is only one talent available for development, and if that talent can only be developed at a particular time, place and under certain constrained conditions. The choice one has when fulfilling one's duty to develop a particular talent for playing the violin, for instance, will be restricted by the conventions and requirements necessary for developing the skills for playing the violin. Therefore, the Kantian moral duty to develop one's talents has the potential to be imperfect *or* perfect, depending on how particular the duty ought to be characterised in order for it to be successfully fulfilled.[21]

2.4.2. Duties to Oneself

---

[21] Accepting that the duty to develop one's talents could be classed as perfect, might result in a worry that the duty is personally over-demanding for an agent. It has been argued that Kant mitigates the worry of moral over-demandingness by allowing an agent some discretion in how to fulfil imperfect duties. If these duties are in fact classified as perfect, then there is no such discretion on behalf of the agent, and as a result, Kant's account of morality could be seen as prescribing duties that are too narrowly specified and count as over-demanding (see Fairbanks: 123-126). For now I leave this issue aside, and in Chapter Four I will discuss in more detail the over-demandingness objection with regards to the moral obligation to develop one's talents.

Kant claims that the moral duty to develop one's talents is a duty that one owes to oneself, because the expression and perfection of one's practical rationality that comes with developing a talent is a necessary part of respecting one's own humanity. However, it could be objected that duties to oneself are not possible, and even if they are, that the duty to develop one's talents is not a duty to oneself but rather a duty that we owe to others. I will now respond to each of these two objections in turn.

First, we might think that duties to oneself are logically impossible due to the relationship that one has with oneself as being insufficient to generate such a duty. Kant seems to recognise the apparent worry here, acknowledging that having a duty to oneself means "we would have to think of ourselves as both being bound by the duty and the one who is doing the binding"; as a result, we might never be truly bound because "the one imposing the obligation could always release the one put under the obligation from the obligation" (MM 6:417-8). To explain, if there is such a thing as a duty to oneself, one would have to both impose the obligation *and* be constrained by the obligation at the same time, which seems impossible. If I impose a duty on someone by making a claim on them, then I have the right to release that person from their duty. However, if I am doing both the imposing and constraining, then I would always have the opportunity to release myself from the duty as and when I desire; this makes having a duty to myself impossible, as a duty is something one should not be able to release oneself from (Singer 1959; Paton 1990: 225).

This objection can be responded to by recognising that it misconstrues what it means to be able to 'release' someone from their duty. The reason why a duty is imposed on us is because it is what the Categorical Imperative demands, a demand which is generated and realised by one's own reason. The only ways in which one could possibly be released from a duty is if one (a) realises that one has actually been mistaken, and what one thought was a duty is not in fact a duty after all, such that the Categorical Imperative in fact demands one to act in a different way altogether, or (b) if one performs an action contrary to the duty and violates it, which is not to release oneself from a duty but rather to disregard the duty altogether. Duties aren't generated from the claims of others, but the Categorical Imperative itself (Korsgaard 1998: 68). It is therefore not possible to release oneself from a duty in the way that the objection suggests, and as a result, duties to oneself are logically possible.

Even if duties to oneself are possible in the way just described, we might further object that the duty to develop one's talents need not be a duty that one owes to oneself, but one that we owe to others. On this view, developing one's talents would only be required if doing so would be for the benefit of one's treatment towards others, and would only be morally valuable in terms of one's respect of the moral claims that others make on us. Those who argue along these lines have to demonstrate why the duty to develop one's talents cannot be one that one owes to oneself, and it is not clear why we need to accept such a claim.

Kant claims that the moral worth of developing one's talents is grounded in the respect for humanity, and this requires treating all moral agents as equally valuable. Failing to treat ourselves as equally valuable in this way would be to disrespect ourselves as less morally worthy than any other moral agent (Eisenberg: 144; Denis: 326, 334; Paton: 224). It seems right that we should value and treat ourselves with the same respect that we would give to others. However, one consequence of this would be that even if there is only one person in existence, Kant would still claim that this person is a moral agent and have duties that are deemed as *moral* duties. Take the example used in the previous chapter, of the one-person world in which an agent has high levels of potential for musical ability. If we could assess that this person has a talent for music, then Kant would be able to claim that she has a duty to develop her talent, and that this duty is a moral one because it is indexed to the respect that she has for her own humanity.

It could be objected that morality is just a social phenomenon, such that morality merely concerns the sphere of one's behaviours and actions that affect others (Eisenberg: 129). Kurt Baier, for example, claims that morality results from the connections, relationships and interactions that we have with other people, and that morality has no relevance in situations where there is no 'other' to interact with: a "world of Robinson Crusoes has no need for a morality and no use for one" (Baier: 215; Denis: 321-323). However, Kant has no reason to accept this claim; he can also be interpreted as claiming that morality is inherently social, especially as expressed in his final formulation of the Categorical Imperative where he states that morality involves the deliberation of rational agents. Even though morality is social and grounded in social claims in this way, this does not necessarily mean that the way we treat ourselves cannot count as a moral interaction, because we ought to value and respect ourselves in the same way that we respect others, as moral agents.

It is irrelevant whether we call this kind of respect for oneself as 'moral' respect or 'ethical' respect, or some other kind of respect altogether; what is important is the idea that the name points to, which is the claim that we ought to respect our own humanity, even if doing so does not affect the claims that others make on us. As such, the duty to develop one's talents can be thought of as a duty that is owed to oneself, and in Kant's account of morality, this duty, grounded in respect for our humanity, is termed as a *moral* duty because it is generated by the Categorical Imperative. This is not just because the duty that we have to respect our humanity acts as the condition of possibility for moral agency more generally, but also because it is a duty that demands of us to treat ourselves as moral agents with equal moral worth. In order to reject Kant's claim, the burden of proof thus lies on those who assume that morality necessarily has to be defined solely as a social phenomenon and consequently that this means morality cannot involve requirements about how individuals treat themselves are moral agents.

2.4.3. The Moral Priority of Talent Development

I have so far proposed that the duty to develop one's talents should be thought of as a duty to oneself that is neither perfect nor imperfect exclusively, but is to be fulfilled by each agent with the right amount of choice as the situation requires. Even with these qualifications in place, I argue that Kant cannot plausibly claim that there is a moral duty to develop one's talents. This is because Kant does not successfully demonstrate that there is a moral priority attached to developing specifically one's talents, as opposed to any other competencies or non-talent abilities that one may have.

Kant claims that a talent is an advantageous "natural gift", "excellence" and "fortunate natural predisposition" (Anthropology: 115). From this we can assume that Kant considers a talent to be more than a general capacity for any kind of competency or behaviour. For example, I may have the capacity to run, but this does not mean that I have a *talent* for running; in Chapter One I argued that for someone to be talented, their capacity or mere ability ought to be something that is expressed in the above-average or excellent acquisition of that particular skill. Kant seems to offer a similar account of talents, or at least one that is compatible with my account, which understands talents as attributed to those who exhibit some excellence in their skill acquisition which is beyond the norm. This is made clear when Kant claims that talents are fortunate and advantageous dispositions.

With this understanding of the nature of talents in mind, the Formula of Universal Law looks like it can't generate a moral duty to develop specifically one's talents, but rather it generates the weaker claim that one ought to develop any capacity that will contribute to one being able to fulfil one's goals, whatever they happen to be. Universalising the maxim that I neglect to develop the skills in which I demonstrate an excellent level of acquisition and development does not necessarily contradict the Categorical Imperative in conception or in willing. In order to be provided with the goods I need for a flourishing life, I do not need others to be *talented* pizza makers or beer crafters, or artists, or healthcare professionals; I only require that they have developed their skills to a level of adequate competency so that they can provide me with the relevant and necessary goods.

The universalisation test does not justify the claim that we ought to *perfect* the useful capacities that we need in order to promote the good life or a flourishing society, but only that we develop our skills to the required competency that is necessary for society to function productively. This means that there is no irrationality involved in failing to develop one's talents, but only one's competencies. And so, according to the Formula of Universal Law, there is no duty to develop or perfect one's talents, but only one's capacities more generally; there would be nothing morally wrong about choosing to develop a skill in which one is merely competent.

The Formula of Humanity is similarly unable to provide the reasons for why there is moral duty to develop specifically one's talents. Kant prescribes that we ought to develop our talents because they allow one to excellently express and perfect one's own humanity – one's rational capacity to set ends and adopt the means necessary for those ends. But it is not clear why it is the perfection specifically of one's talents, rather than any other competencies that one might have, that necessarily expresses and perfects these rational capacities.

For example, it might be that I have a talent for playing the violin, but despite this I really enjoy studying mathematics even though I'm not considered to be a talented mathematician according to the relevant comparative thresholds set by society. Nonetheless, I work extremely hard in my mathematical studies, working to perfect all the capacities in me that will allow me to become a successful mathematician, but in doing so I have to neglect my talent for playing the violin. The Formula of Humanity gives us no reason to believe that I have a moral duty to develop my talent for playing the violin rather than my capacity to be a mathematician. As long as I am expressing and respecting my humanity by exercising my practical reason and improving upon it, then for Kant there can be no moral differentiation made between talents and mere competencies. As a result, we cannot conclude from Kant's Categorical Imperative, that it would be a moral failing to neglect the development of our talents as long as we are nurturing our humanity in other ways.

This argument depends on the assumption that we would always be able to choose between developing our talents and developing some other competency that similarly expresses and develops the perfection of our humanity. It might be the case, however, that you choose to neglect your talent for playing the violin, and this results in neglecting the development of your rational capacities altogether – such a maxim would not work to promote and respect your humanity. In this situation Kant would prescribe that you ought to promote and respect your humanity; if developing your talent for playing the violin was the only way to do this, then you ought to develop that talent. This only means that we would be required by morality to develop our talents if it was found that developing all of our other competencies would not result in the perfection of our rational capacities.

It is also important to remember that Kant does not just state that we should perfect only a few of our capacities, but "all the capacities" in us and to the highest possible standard that we can (GW 4:423). This means that if I only had one capacity, and this happened to be a talent for playing the violin, then I would have a moral duty to develop that talent insofar as it is the only way for me to fulfil my duty to respect my humanity. This is an extremely strong claim, however, and it is almost impossible to imagine a situation in which this binary tension would arise, between developing my one talent, or not being able to fulfil my moral duty; functioning properly as a rational moral agent requires many different and often mundane capacities that we take for granted in everyday life, such as talking, writing, and listening. Although everyone does not have all and the same capacities, it would be strange to imagine someone without any of these general capacities yet still exhibiting a talent for, say, playing the violin, sprinting or painting. As a result, developing one's talents does not seem like the only way in which to respect and perfect one's humanity.[22]

In response to this objection, it could be suggested that Kant's duty of respect for humanity actually *does* entail that developing one's talents is morally superior to developing one's mere competencies. The requirement that we respect our humanity necessitates that we respect what is valuable about ourselves and what is excellent in us. Considering that Kant understands that we ought to respect the parts of us that are central to our humanity, then as part of our duty to perfect humanity we necessarily ought to develop those capacities in us which most excellently develops and perfects our rationality. Talents seem to be the most likely candidate for this, as they are dispositional qualities that manifest in the excellent acquisition of a particular skill, and are also the

---

[22] Against my objection it could be argued that Kant does not claim that we have a general duty to develop our talents above all other alternatives, but merely that we have a duty not to sit idly by rather than develop our talents. However, even if this is the case, (the textual evidence I have given in this Chapter seems to suggest otherwise), and Kant is merely claiming that we should not be lazy and waste our lives in idleness, it is not clear why Kant then argues that to remedy this we ought to develop our talents. My claim is that competencies will do just fine to secure the requirement that arises from the Formula of Humanity, to preserve and perfect our rational capacities. The duty of self-perfection that stems from the requirement not to be lazy or idle, does not necessarily involve the requirement to develop our talents. Developing mere competencies will suffice.

expression of multiple capacities. For example, if someone has a talent for playing tennis, this means that they will excellently acquire the skill, and in doing so develop various capacities, such as moving one's body quickly and efficiently, having good coordination, competitive spirit, and mental endurance. Because developing one's talent exhibits many capacities at once, and these capacities are ones that are manifested in excellent skill acquisition, it could be argued that one's talent best fulfils the requirement to respect and perfect one's rationality.

It is not clear, however, or at least we should not take it for granted, that developing one's talents does count as an excellence in this way. To begin with, it is not obvious that developing one's talents is a moral excellence, partly because a person could have a talent for a skill that we determine to be morally wrong if exhibited in certain ways, for example, a skill for lock-picking or utilising a gun in order to cause harm. It might be that the development of those skills is useful for promoting practical reason, and thus respecting humanity, but it is not the case that expressing that talent is in fact morally worthy, insofar as it fails to respect the humanity of others, and may even result in their harm. If this is the case, then it is hard to see why there would be a moral duty to develop these morally impermissible skills, just because they excellently perfect one's rational capacities.

Furthermore, it is not clear why it is specifically our talents, as opposed to our mere competencies, that excellently promote and perfect one's rationality. It could be the case that given the particulars of a situation, it is actually the development of one's mere competencies that perfects one's rationality, rather than one's talents. If someone begins to develop a skill at a lower level of competency, then they will need to work hard and overcome challenges in order to develop that skill to a high standard. This will require a person to consistently set ends and adopt the means to pursue those ends, and as such, constantly work to preserve and perfect their rational capacities throughout the development of the skill. Someone who is talented, by contrast, will find the acquisition of the particular skill comes more easily and quickly, without the need to challenge and develop their rational capacities. In some situations at least, it will therefore be the development of our mere capacities rather than our talents that will most likely work to respect and perfect our rational capacities. As a result, Kant cannot take for granted the moral priority of talents over other abilities or competencies when explicating why we have a moral duty to develop our talents. In fact, there is good reason to suggest that talents, understood as excellences, are not more valuable or desirable when it comes to respecting our rationality and humanity. Therefore, the duty that we have to perfect our humanity does not require that we ought to develop specifically our talents, but rather that we ought to develop any competencies we may have that will serve to enhance and develop our rational capacities. Even if moral agency is generated by the development of practical rationality, I argue that this does not rely on the development of our talents.

2.5. Conclusion

In this chapter I have argued against Kant's claim that there is a moral duty to develop one's talents. This means that if we do have a moral obligation to develop our talents, then it cannot be justified in terms of Kant's account of morality. I began by analysing the two arguments that Kant gives in support of his claim, as found in his Formula of Universal Law and the Formula of Humanity. I then discussed three objections that could be raised against Kant's account. First, I argued that the duty to develop one's talents is not necessarily imperfect, as Kant claims, but also has the potential to be a perfect duty. This is because the difference between an imperfect and perfect duty is not one of kind but of degree. I noted that because the duty to develop one's talents may be perfect, this would mean that the duty does not allow for any free choice from the agent as to how she will fulfil her duty. Second, I responded to the objection that the duty to develop one's talents should not be thought of as a duty to oneself, but rather as a duty that we owe to others. I argued that duties to oneself are indeed logically possible, and furthermore, that there is no good reason why the duty to develop ones' talents should not be thought of as a moral duty that is owed to oneself; this duty is generated by the Categorical Imperative and the requirement that we ought to respect our own humanity and moral worth.

Finally, I argued that Kant does not succeed in explaining why developing talents is morally superior to developing any other competencies that we may have. The Formula of Universal Law only provides justification for the claim that we ought to develop our skills to the required level of competency so as to avoid a contradiction in willing. Similarly, it is not clear why the Formula of Humanity requires the development specifically of our talents; this is because developing one's competencies is often more likely to more fully and consistently perfect one's rational capacities, and furthermore, we would always be able to choose between developing our talents and developing some other competency that would express and perfect our rational capacities.

Kant cannot successfully claim that developing one's talents is morally superior to developing one's competencies when it comes to adhering either to the Formula of Universal Law or the Formula of Humanity. As a result, Kant does not succeed in arguing that one has an imperfect moral duty to oneself to develop one's talents. In the next chapter I will go on to discuss two further theories that make explicit claims regarding the obligations and reasons we have to develop our talents. I will argue that moral perfectionism is equally unable to generate the claim that we have a moral obligation to develop our talents, and that welfare perfectionism cannot successfully claim that we have good prudential reasons to do so.

Chapter Three

Perfectionism, Excellence and Endorsement

3.1. Introduction

In the last chapter, I concluded that given the commitments of Kant's moral theory, he cannot successfully claim that there is a moral obligation to develop one's talents. Kant considered talent development as necessary for the perfection of one's human rationality and moral agency, however, I argued that Kant fails to generate the moral priority of talents over mere competencies. As a result, we have no reason to consider the development of our talents to be morally required of us, at least by appealing to Kant.

The reason for focussing on Kant's moral philosophy was guided by the fact that unlike many other moral theories, Kant makes an explicit claim about the necessary connection between talent development and moral agency. It is not only Kant's moral theory, however, that makes an explicit claim about the relationship between talent development and morality. Moral perfectionism makes a similar claim, that talent development expresses and promotes the perfection of human flourishing and moral development, and as a result, there is a self-regarding moral obligation to develop one's talents (Hurka: 17-18, 56, 194).

In this chapter, I argue that moral perfectionists cannot plausibly generate the moral obligation to develop one's talents from the commitments of their theory. This is because developing one's talents is not objectively morally good in the way that perfectionists claim, as there is no support for understanding the development of one's talents as an 'excellence'. I call this the 'excellence' objection. If this objection holds, then it means that we cannot plausibly claim there is a *pro tanto* moral obligation to develop one's talent by appealing to moral perfectionism.

Perfectionism, however, has another aspect to it. Some perfectionists do not consider their account of human flourishing to be a moral theory, but rather an account of the nature of well-being and prudential goods. This type of perfectionist, the 'welfare' perfectionist, does not claim that there is a moral obligation to develop one's talents, but rather that developing one's talents is objectively prudentially good for an agent (Kraut: 45-47). This means that according to welfare perfectionism, developing one's talent is considered to be a constitutive part of an agent's well-being, insofar as it manifests and promotes excellent human flourishing.

In this chapter, I also argue that welfare perfectionism is similarly subject to the excellence objection; the theory does not successfully prove that there is a *pro tanto* prudential reason to develop one's talents. Furthermore, given that the theory is an account of well-being, I argue that it is also subject to another objection that is specifically targeted against the claim that talent development counts as an objective *prudential* good. I propose that if the development of one's talents is to be regarded as a constitutive part of an agent's well-being, it is conditional on the agent's endorsement of that development. I will go on to explain this endorsement in terms of a 'constraint' on all theories of well-being, and argue that if this endorsement constraint is not met, then developing one's talents is not prudentially good. From this I finally conclude that both the moral and welfare varieties of perfectionism fail to successfully support their claims regarding the necessary connection between talent development and human flourishing.

In Section Two I begin by outlining the commitments held by both moral and welfare perfectionism, focussing on the arguments they offer for considering talent development to be objectively good and a constitutive part of one's human flourishing. In section Three I introduce the 'excellence objection', arguing against the perfectionist's claim that talent development most excellently constitutes the flourishing of our essential human capacities. As a result, talent development cannot be considered as an objective perfectionist good. In Section Four I turn specifically to welfare perfectionism, and present two examples in which it seems as if the development of one's talent is not an objective prudential good. In Section Five I explain that these examples rely on the intuition that talent development can only be prudentially good for an agent if it fits with the agent's deeply held normative commitments. Without this fit, what is deemed to be prudentially good for an agent will in fact be alienating. After discussing how hybrid versions of perfectionism have attempted to avoid this worry of alienation, in Section Six I argue that if talent development is to 'fit' with an agent's deep normative commitments, then it must be endorsed by the agent – this is what I call the 'endorsement constraint'. Before concluding in Section Seven, I respond to objections that can be raised against my formulation of the endorsement constraint, and claim that endorsement is indeed necessary when determining whether an agent has a *pro tanto* prudential reason to develop her talents.

3.2. Perfectionism and Talent Development

3.2.1. The Fundamental Claim

Both moral and welfare perfectionists share the same core claim, that human flourishing is a fundamental objective good, and that this flourishing consists in the excellent development, exercise and realisation of one's essential human capacities. What counts as a person's essential human capacities is defined in terms of what it means to be human – that which identifies humans as humans as opposed to any other species. As Dorsey concisely puts it, "[t]he good for an *x* is determined by the core account of what it means to be an *x*" (Dorsey 2012: 62).

The exact details of what counts as an essential human capacity varies according to the particular type of perfectionism. Thomas Hurka, for example, claims that human nature consists in the three Aristotelian essential properties of physicality, theoretical rationality and practical rationality (Hurka: 37). Robert Kraut, by contrast, advocates one's cognitive, affective, sensory and social powers as being among the intuitive list of natural human capacities (Kraut: 137), whilst T. H. Green claims that our human nature is necessarily grounded in our moral agency, such that what defines us as humans is that which makes moral agency possible – our deliberative capacity for practical rationality (Green: 183-200; Dorsey 2012: 63).

Whatever is decided upon as being a human's essential capacities, the perfectionist will claim that the excellent development of those capacities is what constitutes human flourishing, and that nurturing these capacities is objectively good.[23] Given this fundamental claim, perfectionism comes in two main varieties. First, moral perfectionism states that human flourishing is not just objectively good, but that it is *the* objective moral good. This means that we have fundamental and unconditional moral reasons to perfect our central human capacities (Hurka: 3). Second, welfare perfectionism does not claim that human flourishing is a moral good, but instead it considers the perfection of one's essential human capacities to be an unconditional and objective *prudential* good, constitutive of one's well-being (Kraut: 74-5). As such, both moral and welfare perfectionism are objective theories. They claim that the value of human flourishing is objective, in the sense that what makes human flourishing good and confers goodness onto the development of human nature, does not rely on an agent's own attitude towards that flourishing and development (Dorsey 2012: 61; Ferkany: 472-3). For the moral perfectionist this objective goodness is a moral good, and for the welfare perfectionist this objective goodness is a prudential good.

Not only do different types of moral and welfare perfectionism vary according to how they define what counts as an essential human capacity, but they also differ in how they deem the perfection and development of these capacities to be fulfilled. Both Hurka and Kraut, for example, initially seem to propose a maximising view, which claims that one's essential capacities should be

---

[23] There are some versions of perfectionism that do not rely specifically on an account of essential human capacities, but rather claim that the excellent life is one in which we maximise or achieve excellence in certain areas of life, objectively specified and without reference to what makes us essentially human. For example, Rawls claims that these perfectionist goods are "art, science and culture" (Rawls 1999: 286), and Humboldt claims that the objective good in question is 'individuality', such that an agent ought to aim for "the integration and development of the various talents they possess" (Humboldt 1986, cited in Colburn 2010: 15). Griffin (1988) and Arneson (2000), for example, both specify their own objective lists describing what counts as an excellent objective good. Although I do not deal with these accounts of perfectionism specifically, much of what I say in this chapter against perfectionism will be relevant to these other accounts; noticeably, my claim that developing one's talents does not necessarily result in the excellent demonstration of these objective perfectionist goods, whatever they may be and irrespective of whether they are defined in terms of human nature.

developed maximally and to the full. Hurka states that "the best perfectionism is a maximising consequentialism", advocating that our human capacities "are pursued to the highest degree" and aim at "full human development" (Hurka: 55-6, 63). Kraut claims that we are truly flourishing when we are "developing properly and fully [...] making full use of [our] potentialities, capacities and faculties" (Kraut: 131). On this reading, it is the full and maximal development of our central human capacities that is constitutive of our human flourishing. However, both Hurka and Kraut qualify that this maximisation ought to be expressed appropriately across one's set of capacities; we ought to aim for a balanced, well-rounded life that does not emphasise the development of one capacity over another. As such, human flourishing consists in the appropriate realisation and balanced development of all of our essential human capacities (Kraut: 170-172; Hurka: 91; Kaupinnen: 3).

For the purposes of this chapter I am going to leave aside any objections that might be associated with these maximising and balancing versions of perfectionism, as well as any objections that can be raised against perfectionism's understanding of what counts as an essential part of human nature – there have been numerous criticisms of perfectionism for these reasons (Dorsey 2010; Kitcher 1999; Haybron 2007). In what follows I grant the perfectionist her account of well-being or morality as consisting in the excellent development of human nature, however this may be described, and I focus on the perfectionist's assertion that developing specifically one's *talents* is objectively good. I will now go on to explain why perfectionists consider talent development to be a constitutive part of the excellent development of one's human nature.

3.2.2. Talents and Human Flourishing

According to perfectionism, talent development is objectively good because it is a constitutive part of the excellent development of one's human nature, and is necessary for the perfection of one's essential human capacities. In Chapter One

I proposed an account of the nature of talents that initially seems to explain the perfectionist's consideration of talents as an excellence in this way. I claimed that talents are a high level of potential for a skill that is excellently manifested in the ease and speed with which that skill is acquired. This proficiency will allow the talented person to reach a higher standard of skill than someone who is not talented, if that talent is properly developed. For example, William may have the capacity to sing, but this does not mean that he has a *talent* for singing; for someone to be talented, they not only need the initial capacity or ability, but that capacity ought to be expressed in the above-average, or 'excellent' development of that skill. This makes sense of the way in which we consider the relevant skills as coming 'naturally' to those who are talented.

It therefore seems as if talents are the best candidate for the realisation of the requirement to perfect one's central human capacities. Those who are talented are more likely to achieve 'excellent' human development, as their talents enable their capacities to be developed more efficiently and productively. In this way, developing one's talent is to engage in the excellent development and perfection of one's human flourishing – the more you develop your talents, the more you will promote the expression and development needed to achieve this flourishing.

To illustrate this point, Hurka gives the example of a talented scientist, claiming that the scientist's talent "is what is best in her and what she should most strive to develop" (Hurka: 27). Hurka claims not only that one's talent is worth developing, but also that one has a moral *obligation* to develop one's talents. He writes that, "the duty to develop one's talents is more pressing for those with greater talents. [...] We could not say of someone who was content with a reasonable development of his talents that he aimed at "excellence" or was dedicated to "perfecting" himself" (Hurka: 56). From this it is clear that Hurka considers only the full development of one's talents to be indicative of excellence and the perfection of one's human nature, whilst the failure to develop one's talents or the mere adequate development of a talent lacks this excellence. [24]

When it comes to welfare perfectionism, Kraut similarly claims that developing one's talents is a constitutive part of one's human flourishing. Although this does not amount to giving one a *moral* reason to develop one's talents, Kraut does claim that one has an objective *prudential* reason to do so. Kraut gives the example of a young person who has the "talents that would make a medical career the best career for him", and that developing those talents "is something he should want and should pursue because it would be good for him that he do so" (Kraut: 112-3). Kraut considers the development of the young person's medical talents to be in his best interest and a constitutive part of his well-being, irrespective of the young person's own attitudes and evaluative perspective. Initially it might seem that Kraut's formulation gives some weight to one's wants and desires – Kraut writes that the development of the person's talents is something that he should *want*. However, the person's pro-attitudes are not what *makes* the development of his talents good for him, but rather, as Kraut makes explicit, the agent should desire such development *because* it is good for him, and would be good for him even if he had no such desire.

Therefore, perfectionists make a strong claim, that what makes something morally or prudentially good is that it promotes the perfection of our human nature. Talent development is objectively good in this way, due to the fact that it not only promotes, but is a constitutive part of, the excellent development of our essential human capacities. It is the perfectionist's emphasis on the objective

---

[24] It is important to note that for Hurka, merely *aiming* for the full and excellent development of one's talents would suffice. It might be, for whatever reason, that the scientist in Hurka's example does not achieve her goal for the full development of her scientific talents, but it is the fact that she aims for this goal and adopts the means to achieve it that counts as an instance of perfect development. The emphasis for the perfectionist is the active process of development, rather than the finished end of a certain capacity being developed. This is highlighted by the fact that Hurka laments the person who is content with the average development of her talents, suggesting that the perfectionist good is compromised when one fails to adopt the appropriate means and attitudes necessary for bringing about one's excellent development. It is another question altogether whether or not Hurka's claim here is compatible with his assertion that moral perfectionism is a version of maximising consequentialism.

moral and prudential goodness of talent development that I put pressure on in the rest of this chapter. In what follows I object to the perfectionist claim that talent development necessarily and objectively contributes to the excellent development of one's central human capacities. I argue that there is in fact no support for considering talent development to be objectively 'excellent' in this way.

3.3. The Excellence Objection

Perfectionists claim that the development of one's talents is constitutive of the excellent and perfect development of one's essential human capacities. However, given the commitments of perfectionism, I argue that the theory is unable to generate the evaluative priority of talent development over the development of one's other abilities and competencies; talent development is not 'excellent' in the way that perfectionists prescribe. This is for two reasons: (i) talents do not necessarily realise the perfection of one's essential human capacities, and (ii) talents are not necessary morally good. I will deal with each in turn.

3.3.1. Talents and Essential Human Capacities

It is not always true that the development of one's talents will necessarily realise the perfection of one's central human capacities. In which case, there is no reason for the perfectionist to favour or give priority to the development of one's talents over one's competencies and non-talents. To explain, refer back to the account of talents raised in Chapter One. The nature of a talent is such that it manifests itself in the excellent acquisition of a particular skill; for someone who is talented, their development will come more naturally to them, allowing them to more easily reach a higher standard of skill than those who are not talented. But this ease of development may entail that the talented person does not in fact excellently develop their essential human capacities in the way that the perfectionist requires. In fact, it may be that the talented person actually uses and develops *fewer* of her central human capacities, simply because she does not need to develop them in order to achieve a high level of success for a particular skill.

This can be illustrated by an example. Two friends, Freya and Claire, are both developing their violin-playing abilities. It turns out that Freya is a talented violinist and finds that developing the necessary skills comes naturally to her, but Claire on the other hand is not a talented violinist, and finds developing her abilities rather challenging. In order to reach the same level of skill, Freya, for instance, will only have to practice for half an hour a day and finds this practice easy, whereas Claire has to practice intensely and with difficulty for two hours per day.

I suggest that it is in fact Claire, not Freya, who is developing and perfecting her essential human capacities more fully, because in order to develop her skill, Claire perseveres through challenging, hard work. In most perfectionist accounts, practical rationality is claimed to be an essential human capacity, allowing a person to set coherent goals and adopt the effective means in order to achieve these goals. In order to develop and perfect this capacity, a person will, amongst other things, have to cultivate and exhibit virtues such as perseverance, patience, understanding and focus, as well as developing an understanding of who one is, how one learns, and what one's limits are. These epistemic virtues are often only nurtured if a person encounters and has to overcome challenges and hard work, and this is not often the case if a skill comes easily and does not require perseverance, patience and reflection. Therefore, it is often the development of our mere competencies rather than the development of our talents that will work to perfect the capacity for practical rationality, allowing for the opportunity to overcome difficulty.[25] Because Claire has had to develop her violinist skills from a lower level of competency, and as a result will have had to work hard, persevere and be challenged further as she develops that skill, she will as a consequence nurture more fully her essential human capacity for practical rationality.[26]

---

[25] Gwen Bradford has recently offered an account of the value of achievement, stating that part of the value of developing our skills and talents can be found in the fact that doing so is difficult (Bradford 2013).

[26] In fact, Hurka himself claims that the perfection of human flourishing ought to include "challenging activities that are also valued for themselves" (Hurka: 128). If my argument holds, and talents do not embody this notion of a challenging activity, then Hurka's claims regarding the perfectionist value of challenging activity and the necessary perfectionist good of talent development will be inconsistent.

The perfectionist might object to this point, and claim that if we are concerned about how the ease of one's development may hinder the perfection of one's human capacities, all we need to ensure is that those who are talented challenge themselves to a greater extent, set difficult goals and expend more effort in their development. Talents may still be the best candidate for perfecting one's human nature because they allow a person to more efficiently and productively reach a higher level of skill development, especially if we ensure that those who are talented are given challenges fitting for their level of ability.

However, perfectionists do not merely claim that a person ought to develop her talents because they allow her to achieve high levels of skill acquisition. Their claim is rather that a person ought to develop her talents because doing so allows her to promote the excellent development of her essential human capacities, in order to achieve human flourishing. There is nothing in this claim that points to the quantity of one's achieved skills, indicating that one has to reach the highest possible level of skill. Merely claiming that the development ought to be more difficult seems to be an *ad hoc* move on the part of the perfectionist. The perfection of one's essential human capacities, such as practical rationality, may be excellently developed *without* achieving the highest level of skill. For example, if Freya has a talent for playing the violin, but a mere competency in mathematics, it is not necessarily the development of her violin-playing skills that will work to perfect her human capacity of practical rationality. As outlined above, the challenge and hard-work that she perseveres through in order to develop her competency in mathematics may in fact nurture more fully her practical rationality, and thus her human flourishing.

Furthermore, because talent is a socially relative and comparative phenomenon, as I discussed in Chapter One, there is nothing to say that cultivating one's talents necessarily promotes the excellent development of one's essential human capacities. In Chapter One, I argued for a definition of talents that depends on how one's level of ability and skill acquisition compares to others, and whether or not the skill that is exhibited by the development of one's talent is valued by society. Just because one's ability is valued by society, and one's skill acquisition is determined to be comparatively above average, this does not mean that the development of that ability will necessarily promote the excellent development of one's essential human capacities. For example, it might be that Freya lives in a society that considers her ability for precisely identifying scents to be a talent – the skill is valued by society and her acquisition of the skill is considered to be comparatively excellent. However, just because Freya's scent-identifying ability is labelled as a 'talent', this does not necessarily mean that its development will perfect her essential human capacities of practical and theoretical rationality in a way that is more 'excellent' than the development of her competency for mathematics.

Therefore, just because a particular ability or skill is determined to be a 'talent', this does not mean that it will objectively and necessarily be constitutive of the excellent development of one's essential human capacities. This is because the ease that comes with the development of one's talents might in fact hinder the perfection of one's essential human capacities. Furthermore, the fact that the acquisition of one's skill is comparatively above average and is valued favourably by society does not entail that its development will necessarily and objectively promote the perfection of one's human flourishing. As such, there is no reason for perfectionism to give significance to the development of one's talent over the development of other competencies that one might have.

3.3.2. Talents and Moral Value

The second reason to doubt the perfectionist's claim that developing one's talents is necessarily constitutive of excellent human flourishing, is that a person may have a talent for a skill that we deem to be morally impermissible in some way. It might be that when a skill is developed in certain ways, the skill will give rise to morally blameworthy behaviour – for example, the skill to burgle or lock-pick, or to wield a knife or a gun with the intention to cause harm. The development of such talents may in fact promote one's practical and theoretical reason, or whatever capacity you consider to count as an essential human capacity, but the development of that talent will not be unconditionally and objectively good. In fact, expressing such a talent may seem to lack moral worth and goodness altogether. The perfectionist cannot, as a result, claim that developing *any* talent is good, but only the development of those talents that are considered to be morally permissible. Therefore, developing one's talent is not unconditionally and objectively good or excellent in the way that perfectionism claims, but is conditional on other factors that determine the appropriateness and permissibility of the expression of one's talents.[27]

This objection is more of a problem for moral perfectionism than it is for the welfare perfectionist, because moral perfectionism makes claims about what is unconditionally *morally* good. The fact that developing one's talents can be shown to be only conditionally good, based on other moral considerations that are not derived from the principles of moral perfectionism itself, highlights that the moral perfectionist's claims about the unconditional moral value of talent development are implausible, and that in fact talent development is not always morally good. The welfare perfectionist, by contrast, does not need to make such a claim about the moral good, but instead specifies that developing one's talent is *prudentially* good. In this way, welfare perfectionism is not affected by the objection that developing one's talents may actually be morally wrong.[28]

However, I argue that welfare perfectionism is vulnerable to another objection that has a similar structure to the one just raised against moral perfectionism, that developing one's talents is not always morally good because there are cases in which developing one's talent may be morally wrong. I reject the welfare perfectionist's claim that developing one's talents is prudentially good because there are cases in which developing one's talents may not be prudentially

---

[27] Hurka states that perfectionism is in fact a version of consequentialism, such that we ought to maximise perfection for *all* agents and to promote "the greatest development of human nature by all humans everywhere" (Hurka: 55). This might mean that Hurka has a response to the objection just raised, claiming that if the development of one's talents hinders the promotion of others developing their essential human capacities, then this would not be considered as morally good. However, there still may be circumstances in which developing one's talents *does not* result in the hindrance of another's flourishing, yet still be thought of as immoral due to the harm it may cause. There is nothing to say that all instances of harm to others necessarily results in a lack of their human flourishing, for example, lying to someone need not harm the development of their central human capacities; at least, the burden of proof is on Hurka to prove that we ought to accept this claim.

[28] It might be that what is prudentially good for us *does* incorporate to some extent the concerns of morality. However, this is far from uncontroversial, and for the purposes of the discussion in this chapter all that one needs to admit is that it is not *necessarily* the case that our prudential concerns ought to reflect what is morally permissible or required.

good. We have good reason to doubt the unconditional and objective prudential value of talent development insofar as it may be implausibly alienating for an agent, as I will now discuss.

3.4. Two Intuitive Cases against Perfectionism

Welfare perfectionism claims that developing one's talents is an objective prudential good because doing so most excellently perfects our human nature, and this perfection is constitutive of one's well-being. So, one has a *pro tanto* prudential reason to develop one's talents, and the prudential goodness attached to the development of one's talents is objective – that is, it does not depend on one's attitudes towards doing so. In the remainder of this chapter I argue that this claim is implausible, and that developing one's talents is not necessary and objectively prudentially good. This is because developing one's talents may clash with other normative commitments and fail to constitute part of a person's well-being. I begin to present this objection by exploring two intuitive examples in which it seems that the development of one's talent neither objectively nor necessarily constitutes, or contributes to, an agent's well-being.

3.4.1. The Miserable Philosopher

The first example case is presented by Wayne Sumner, describing a talented philosopher who has up until now pursued a life as a professional philosopher. However, after some consideration, the philosopher realises that he is miserable, and the thought of further pursuing a philosophical career fills him with dread. The philosopher considers himself to be much better-off leading an intellectually unstimulating and laid-back life that fails to exhibit the full development of his talents (Sumner: 24, also cited in Haybron: 7). For sake of argument, let's assume that the philosopher has led an all-things-considered balanced life, with each of his essential human capacities being developed to the amount as deemed appropriate for the perfectionist. Let's also assume that the reason behind the philosopher's negative feelings towards his talent is not motivated by laziness or weakness of will. Instead, what motivates the philosopher's misery is that the further development of his philosophical talent does not engage him in any meaningful way that positively corresponds or contributes to the things that he values in his life. The philosopher's negative attitude towards the development of his talents does not occur as a result of a distorted self-image or an instance of self-sabotage, but due to his considered reflection about who he is, what he values, and the kind of life that he wants for himself.

The perfectionist[29] would claim that what is in fact prudentially good for the philosopher is the full development of his philosophical talent. Failing to further develop his talent will mean that the philosopher's life has less prudential value, and as a result reduces his level of well-being. The example, however, aims to nudge our intuitions by suggesting that the philosopher's misery when continuing to develop his talent casts doubt on whether we would really want to accept that doing so is prudentially good for him. Of course, whether one's misery affects the claim that developing one's talents is prudentially valuable depends on what type of reasons one has for being miserable; I will go on to argue that it is one's lack of endorsement that provides the best reason for thinking that one's misery can refute the claim that talent development is prudentially valuable. Before arguing for this claim, however, I present a second example, which aims to demonstrate the divergence between talent development and well-being without relying on negative emotional reactions like misery, as in this first example.

3.4.2. Multi-talented Mandy

Mandy is lucky to have more than one talent; not only is she a talented creative writer, but she is also a talented tennis player and has a talent for memorising sequences of numbers. Let's also assume that Mandy has so far led a well-balanced life, but unfortunately circumstances are such that now she can only choose to fully develop one of her talents, perhaps due to financial or time constraints.

---

[29] For ease of reference, in this and the proceeding sections of this chapter, I will now use the generic term 'perfectionism' when discussing welfare perfectionism, unless otherwise specified.

Mandy now needs to consider which talent she should develop for her life to go better.

The perfectionist would claim that Mandy should develop the talent that will most excellently promote and perfect her human nature. Depending on the account of human nature offered, different versions of perfectionism will offer different suggestions. For example, Hurka and Green think that the development of one's practical and theoretical rationality constitutes one's human flourishing, in which case Mandy should to develop the talent which is considered to best promote her practical or theoretical rationality. Given that Mandy can only choose one talent, the perfectionist's decision might be based on the skill for which she has the most talent and thus displays most excellence; Mandy might be slightly more talented at playing tennis and so be able to achieve more perfection and excellence from its development than if she developed her creative writing skills. It might also be that Mandy's ability to memorise sequences of numbers is deemed to be less expressive of human development; for example, it may utilise fewer processes of complex ability, or have less chance of being excellently developed and improved. In this case, the perfectionist would recommend that Mandy only develop her number-memory skills if no other option were available to her. This, however, is speculative; the right answer for the perfectionist would depend on the empirical facts about Mandy's talents and what they can offer for the full and excellent development of her essential human capacities.

The crucial point is that perfectionism fails to ask the question that most of us would ask, I think, when trying to decide which talent Mandy should develop. Instead of merely determining what would exhibit the most perfection of her human nature, we would ask which talent Mandy wants to develop, or, which talent would be most fitting for Mandy's personality and what she considers to be of value in her own life. The perfectionist, however, considers the development of a talent as good for Mandy *simpliciter*, without giving enough or any importance to how that development fits with Mandy's own conception of the good life. This ignores Mandy's own capacity to assess her set of talents in relation to her own values and what she determines to be good. As a result, perfectionism has the potential to prescribe the development of a talent as being prudentially good for Mandy, even though it may conflict with her desires or wishes, her conception of the good life, and her fundamental values and commitments. In the next section I argue that for any theory of well-being, this conflict should be avoided due to the fact that it gives rise to the worry of alienation. I conclude that perfectionism, as it stands, is unsuccessful in its attempts to avoid this worry.

3.5. Alienation and Talent Development

3.5.1. Deep Normative Commitments

The two example cases described above highlight the intuition that developing a talent cannot be constitutive of, or contribute to one's well-being if it does not fit with one's sense of self and conception of the good life. As a result, the claim made by perfectionists, that talent development is objectively and necessarily prudentially good for an agent, initially seems to be counter-intuitive. In this section, I argue that the lack of fit between talent development and one's own personal commitments is indeed worrying for perfectionism, because without this fit, the development of one's talent will in fact turn out to be 'alienating' (Rosati 1996: 289-9; Railton 2003: 47). This worry of alienation poses a serious challenge for objectivist theories of well-being, and I argue that in order to avoid the challenge that alienation poses, a theory of well-being must only prescribe prudential goods that fit with an agent's sense of self and conception of the good life and insofar, not alienating. In what follows I will explain in more detail what constitutes this worry of alienation when it comes to talent development, but before I do there are two initial qualifications to make.

First, when it is claimed that an agent's good must fit with their 'sense of self', this is not a reference to a metaphysical notion of selfhood or personal identity. Instead, we are referring to a person's normative conception of themselves and the values that they hold. This is why it is often claimed that the fit in question is between an agent's good and their conception of the good life – that is, what one values and what one deems to be normatively significant in one's life. For example, Korsgaard claims that this normative self should be understood "as a description under which you find your life to be worth living and your actions to be worth undertaking" (Korsgaard 1996: 83), and Carbonell simply explains it as one's "personality" (Carbonell: 5). As such, one's sense of self is that which dictates the values that one adopts as part of the good life, and provides one with reasons for action as a result of these values.

The second qualification to make is to tighten the notion of what counts as the kind of value with which one's good should fit in order for it not to be alienating. It might be, for example, that one's good often conflicts with trivial desires and commitments. For example, the good that comes with being a caring and attentive parent may sometimes conflict with one's passing desire to be unburdened by children, so that one can go out with friends or take a quiet holiday retreat. However, this type of desire is not the kind of thing that a plausible version of well-being would require to fit with an agent's prudential good (Yelle: 372). If it was, then this would mean that what constitutes one's well-being ought to fit with and satisfy all kinds of trivial and fleeting desires, such as a spur of the moment whim for ice-cream, a spontaneous and uncharacteristic aggressive reaction, or a fleeting desire to be child-free just for one night in order to get some sleep. This result would make for a highly unattractive account of the nature of well-being, because it would mean that one's trivial desires could legitimately trump goods that are considered to have significant prudential value.

Instead, I propose that the kind of values that we should refer to as constituting one's sense of self are those that determine an agent's deep normative commitments and shape her conception of the good life, giving significance to objects and states of affairs that are deeply meaningful in her life. These deep commitments are not mere preferences or interests, the satisfaction of which is convenient and good for an agent at the time (Moseley: 60). Instead, they are commitments "around which our lives are organised" (Scheffler 1992: 123) and bestow our lives with meaning and significance; they "lend meaning and importance to the agent's life, and it is under this description that they are perceived as important and authoritative" (Bagnoli: 5, see also Rivera: 71). As such, these commitments persist and play a functional role in shaping and constituting who we are and the values that we consider to be authoritative over our lives. With this qualification in mind, my claim is that in order to avoid the worry of alienation, a theory of well-being must only prescribe prudential goods that fit with an agent's deep normative commitments.

In a theory that doesn't posit this fit between an agent's good and her deeply held normative commitments, what is thought to be prudentially good for that agent has the potential to conflict with her sense of self and conception of the good life. This tension is described by Railton as a form of alienation, "a kind of estrangement, distancing, or separateness (not necessarily consciously attended to) resulting in some sort of loss" (Railton 1984: 134). For the purposes of my argument, I suggest that we use the word 'alienation' as a term of art, to denote the negative implications of a lack of fit between an agent's good and her deep normative commitments when it comes to developing her talents. To be alienated from one's deep normative commitments just means that one will have to forgo and compromise something that is a significant and a meaningful part of one's life.

The loss that is experienced due to this lack of fit can be explained in various ways. For example, Brink explains this loss as grounded in the value of authenticity; he claims that authenticity requires acting on ideals that the agent accepts and in doing so means that she is 'faithful' to the values that form who she is and the kind of person that she wants to be (Brink: 215, 239). Chappell, on the other hand, refers to the value of integrity, understood as being honest about what one values and refusing to compromise those values (Chappell: 256),[30] whilst Rosati explains the loss in terms of a reduction in autonomy, such that the agent is no longer guided by her own values and what she considers to be important in her life (Rosati 2006: 43-44).[31]

---

[30] Dworkin too appeals to the notion of 'integrity': "A life lived with integrity is lived according to our own personal ethical conviction. When others intervene to induce us to live lives that we regret or fail to endorse, they intrude on the integrity of our lives" (Dworkin 2000: 244, see also 248-249 and 270-274). Bernard Williams also appeals to the value of integrity (see Williams 1981).

[31] Ben Colburn similarly appeals to the connection between endorsement and autonomy, as "a value which consists in an agent deciding for herself what is valuable, and living her life in accordance with that decision, where that amounts to an agent successfully pursuing values, which she endorses under conditions of judgemental independence. It is central to this conception of autonomy that it consists in individuals not just shaping their

These three accounts appeal to different values to explain the loss experienced when an agent is alienated from what is considered to be prudentially good for her. What these accounts have in common is the claim that when a state of affairs does not fit with one's deep normative commitments, then acting to bring about that state of affairs can conflict with one's own ideals and compromise the values that determine who one is. So, when a person acts according to a conception of the good that she does not value as part of or complimentary to her deeply held ideals and commitments, this means that there is a conflict and tension with those significant and meaningful parts of her life. Acting contrary to one's deeply held normative commitments will result in alienation, and this alienation counts as a loss in well-being; it is this loss of well-being that renders alienation problematic for a theory of well-being. It seems implausible that a theory of well-being will claim something to be a constitutive part of one's prudential good, even though it has the potential to significantly reduce one's level of well-being. I will now go on to explain how this alienation can occur with regards to the development of one's talents.

3.5.2. Internal and External Commitments

Alasdair MacIntyre makes a distinction between the internal and external goods that come with certain practices. This distinction can be adapted to explain the way in which developing one's talents may conflict with one's deeply held normative commitments. I argue that the practice of developing a talent can result in a conflict with one's deep normative commitments with regards to both the internal and external commitments that are necessarily required when bringing about the development of that talent.

When we develop a talent there comes with it certain required commitments and standards that have to be met in order to successfully engage in the expression and cultivation of the skill that the talent is indexed to. Some of these commitments are external to the specific talent in question. As MacIntyre terms it, these external commitments are "contingently attached" to the practice

---

own lives through their actions and decision, but also having authority over what counts a success or failure in their lives, in the sense that it is their judgement about what is valuable which sets the relevant standard" (Colburn 2014: 258, see also 267, fn. 14).

"by the accidents of social circumstance" (MacIntyre: 188). For example, it might be that successfully developing one's talent for acting also requires you to be able to cope with the pressures of maintaining a high-profile public life. This is not necessarily required by the specific development of your acting skills, but it may come as a contingent aspect of it, due to the way in which actors are currently given celebrity status. A talented philosopher, by contrast, may have to accept that if she continues to develop her talent then her career will unlikely offer great financial reward. Again, this is not unique to the development of philosophical talent, nor is it a necessary aspect of it, but it is contingently true given the time and place in which the talent is developed.

Some of the practices and standards that come with the development of a talent, however, are unique and inherent to the specific talent that is being cultivated – they are 'internal' to that specific talent, and need to be committed to if one is to engage in its development. MacIntyre uses the example of chess: the internal commitments of the practice of chess are the ones relevant specifically to the game of chess (MacIntyre: 188). The internal commitments necessary for the development of that particular practice specify the "standards of excellence and obedience to rules" that are required to bring about the achievement of that development. When we develop a practice, we enter into this by "accept[ing] the authority of those standards" and "subject [our] own attitudes, choices, preferences and tastes to the standards which currently and partially define the practice" (MacIntyre: 190).

When developing a talent, we will often need to align ourselves not just with the external commitments that come conditionally with the development, but also with the standards that the development of the specific skill requires. For example, when nurturing one's talent for swimming, this will require one to be the kind of person that chooses to wake up early in the morning for practice sessions, change one's diet and body shape, and refuse to engage in certain activities that will hinder one's physical progress. These internal commitments are normative – they give you reasons to act in certain ways and to constrain the choices that you make, rendering you accountable to the standards and values set by those commitments. As such, bringing about the development of one's talent requires certain normative commitments that are both external and internal to the relevant necessary practices.

If the internal and external commitments required for developing one's talent do not fit with one's deep normative commitments, a conflict will arise that has the potential to significantly reduce one's well-being in the ways already described above. It might be that the requirement to maintain a high-profile in public life will conflict with one's deeply held value for privacy; it may be that one's personal project to climb Mount Everest creates friction with the internal time commitments necessary for developing one's musical abilities; or it may be that the development of one's talent will require the neglect of various aspects of one's life that are of deep significance, such as spending time with loved ones and helping those in need. Thus, if the internal and external commitments necessary for bringing about the development of a talent hinder or cause an agent to neglect one's own deep normative commitments, then the development of one's talent is alienating, and will likely result in a loss of well-being.

As it stands, perfectionism is subject to this alienation worry. It claims that developing one's talents is objectively good for us, constitutive of an agent's well-being, even though doing so has the potential to cause an alienating conflict with that agent's deep normative commitments. I will now go on to consider the ways in which perfectionists have attempted to respond to this worry of alienation.

3.5.3. Hybrid Perfectionism

The most successful attempt at avoiding the alienation worry for perfectionism has been to forego a commitment to pure perfectionism and adopt a hybrid view, claiming that an agent's enjoyment or pleasure is necessary for perfectionist well-being; that is, perfectionist activity is only perfect or excellent if it is also enjoyed. In this way, an agent's pro-attitude towards a state of affairs is necessary for that state of affairs to be considered as a constitutive part of her well-being. For example, Robert Adams claims that "what is good for a person is a life characterized by enjoyment of the excellent" (Adams: 93), where what is 'excellent' is determined objectively as a perfectionist good. Similarly, Kraut claims that well-being consists in the enjoyment of using and developing our distinctive human powers, sometimes experienced as when the development of those capacities is "perceive[d] with pleasure" (Kraut: 161, 163).

For both Adams and Kraut, pleasure and enjoyment are a necessary part of what makes something prudentially good for an agent, but are significant only when those pro-attitudes are directed towards, and are for the use of, objective perfectionist goods. As Haybron explains, enjoyment and pleasure are derivatively significant for the hybrid perfectionist, only insofar as they allow a perfectionist good to be realised (Haybron: 13). The hybrid perfectionist will thus maintain that we *ought* to enjoy what is deemed to be objectively good for us, and our enjoyment is merely in the service of promoting those already determined perfectionist goods.[32] With regards to talent development, the claim would be that talent development is objectively valuable in its own right; however, without an agent's pro-attitude toward the development of her talent, then that development doesn't constitute a part of her well-being. This means that we can still claim developing talents is valuable *simpliciter*, but maintain that doing so is prudentially good for an agent only if that agent enjoys it in some way.

This hybrid account would not be accepted by most perfectionists, who claim that well-being is constituted by the objective goodness of the development of one's essential human capacities. This goodness is determined irrespective of any desire, feeling or attitudes that we have towards those goods: an agent's pro-attitude is not necessary for perfectionist activity to be good, but merely acts as a bonus or accompaniment to that activity (Hurka: 27; Haybron: 14; Wilkinson 2003). However, the hybrid account does initially seem more considerate of potential alienation worries, because it considers an agent's positive attitude towards the state of affairs in question to be necessary when determining whether or not talent development constitutes the agent's prudential good. In this case, there is more likely to be a fit with the agent's deep normative commitments.

There is an initial objection to the hybrid perfectionist account as it stands: it is not clear why the enjoyment or pleasure that an agent has towards a state of

---

[32] For further examples of similar hybrid accounts, see Kagan (2009), Darwall (1997); Parfit (1984), Griffin (1986), Raz (1988) and Sumner (1996).

affairs necessarily means that the state of affairs fits with her deep normative commitments. For example, there are many times when developing one's talents is not very enjoyable or pleasurable. In fact, there are times when we detest having to develop our talents, and find engaging in the internal and external commitments frustrating or painful – think of athletes who constantly push their bodies to extreme levels of pain in order to reach maximum levels of fitness, writers who spend days trying to overcome writer's block, and musicians practicing mind-numbingly boring scales and studies so that they master correct technique. It would be a welcome bonus if during these times we found pleasure in doing what we know we ought to, but it's not clear why we have to consider that pleasure as a necessary part of what makes nurturing our talents good for us.

This problem can't be avoided just by stating that the agent must at least be *disposed* to take pleasure in such an activity in the right circumstances, for there is no need for the agent to be disposed to find something pleasurable or enjoyable for it to compliment her deep normative commitments. There is no reason why we should necessarily expect the athlete to be disposed to find pleasurable the extreme pain that he undergoes in order to push his body to the limit, or the writer to be disposed to enjoy the experience of her writer's block, even if that pleasure is to occur only after the fact. As a result, enjoyment and pleasure are the not the right kind of pro-attitude to be included in the hybrid perfectionist view.

Instead, I argue that if hybrid perfectionism is to successfully accommodate the prescription that an account of well-being must fit with an agent's deep normative commitments, the perfectionist ought to include the agent's 'endorsement' of the perfectionist good as a necessary part of the agent's well-being, and not merely 'enjoyment'. In order for something that is considered to have objective perfectionist value to be prudentially good for an agent, that agent must endorse it as part of, or complimentary to, her deep normative commitments. This means that for talent development to be prudentially good for an agent, the agent must endorse the internal and external commitments that are necessary for the realisation of that development. This endorsement is a necessary and constituent part of what makes the talent development prudentially good for the agent. As a result, even though we may accept, for sake of argument, the perfectionist claim that there is intrinsic objective goodness in developing one's talents, we nonetheless consider the *prudential* goodness in developing a talent to depend on an agent's endorsement of it. In the next section I explain in more detail the nature of this endorsement and consider further objections to this modified hybrid perfectionist account.

3.6. The Endorsement Constraint

In the last section I suggested that in order for something that has perfectionist value to be prudentially good for an agent, that agent must endorse it as part of, or complimentary to, her deep normative commitments. Without this endorsement, perfectionism offers a theory of well-being that is potentially alienating. The importance of an agent's endorsement when determining the prudential goodness of talent development can be included into a theory of well-being as a constraint:

> *Endorsement Constraint.* Talent Development T is prudentially good for agent A if and only if A endorses the normative commitments that are necessarily required to bring about T, as part of or complimentary to A's deeply held normative commitments.

In this section I explain and argue for the endorsement constraint, as well as respond to objections that can be brought against it. In doing so, I am considering a possible amendment to welfare perfectionism that potentially allows the theory to deal with the worry of alienation.

3.6.1. Endorsement

An agent's endorsement of what is good for her is a considered reflection about what that agent has reason to value as part of her deep normative commitments and conception of the good life. As such, endorsement is not merely an affective state, but also involves an evaluative judgement and a motivational component. If an agent endorses the development of her talent, she decides and accepts that it is valuable to her, and also forms an intention to commit to developing her talent, making that development a part of her life.

As Joseph Raz explains, an agent's endorsement transforms what might have been an 'impersonal' value into a personal or prudential value. So, for example, if the perfectionist claims that developing one's talent has positive value, without an agent's endorsement this value is merely 'impersonal' and does not say anything about whether developing a talent is good for that particular agent. If an agent endorses the development of her talent, however, it means that she has reflected on the value of the impersonal goodness of doing so, and the way in which that good can be incorporated as part of her own life and her own deep personal commitments. Without this endorsement, what might be an impersonal good, with a positive value indexed to it in some way, is not incorporated into an agent's own life and personal projects, and as such is not prudentially good. In this way, one's endorsement *makes* the development of one's talent prudentially good (see Raz 1986: 288-295; Raz 1999: 63-64).

One way we might amend a theory of well-being in order to incorporate the need for an agent's endorsement, is to shift to a fully subjective theory, stating that what is prudentially good for an agent is completely determined as response-dependent, so that there is no need to appeal to what might have objective impersonal value. In this way, what has prudential value is determined entirely by what an agent endorses. However, for perfectionism to accommodate the worry of alienation and to accommodate an agent's endorsement as that which avoids this alienation, there is no need to adopt a fully subjectivist theory. After all, the endorsement constraint is merely a necessary *constraint*, rather than a full account of the nature of well-being. The endorsement constraint only requires us to accept the following claim: given that talent development has some initial positive value indexed to it, this does not necessarily entail that talent development is prudentially good for a particular agent unless that agent also endorses doing so as part of, or complimentary to, her deeply held normative commitments.

For an agent to endorse the development of her talent, her evaluative judgement must include reflection on whether the internal and external commitments that come with the development of her talent fit with her deeply held normative commitments. For example, whether or not the development of Mandy's artistic talent is prudentially good for her will be determined (at least in part) by whether Mandy endorses the development of that talent. To arrive at a decision on this, Mandy will reflect on whether the commitments that come with developing her talent fit with her own deep normative commitments and conception of the good life.

It might be that Mandy's deep normative commitments clash. For example, perhaps the commitments that come with developing her artistic talent will require her to neglect aspects of her life that also have personal significance, such as spending time with her children. The endorsement constraint, however, does not need to prescribe a decision-making method for each agent to follow in order to resolve such a personal conflict. What the endorsement constraint does amount to is the claim that once the agent has resolved this conflict and decided whether or not developing her talent fits with her deeply held normative commitments, it is the agent's endorsement that constitutes the prudential goodness of the development of her talent. As long as Mandy has good reasons for arriving at the endorsement of her talent development, therefore, it is this endorsement that makes the development of her talent prudentially good for her.

3.6.2. The Correctness Objection

There is one very obvious objection to the endorsement constraint I have just described. A person's judgements about their deep normative commitments and what fits with them can be mistaken and ill-formed. This means that alienating an agent from her deep normative commitments might not be such a bad thing; sometimes alienation will have the good consequence of distancing an agent from a situation that is actually bad for her, highlighting the mistakes that she has made with regards to her own judgement of the situation (Railton 1986: 147).

The beliefs and preferences that inform what we value and endorse can be adapted, distorted, and deformed in various ways. Wilkinson, for example, suggests that there are four categories of mistakes that an agent can make when deciding whether she endorses a particular good: mistakes of fact, value, reasoning, and in the application of judgement (Wilkinson: 196). Even if this list is not exhaustive, the worry still holds; if an agent is mistaken about what is of value, then her well-being cannot plausibly be constituted in part by her own endorsement, as she may have just endorsed *wrongly* (Wall: 197). For ease, I will call this objection the 'correctness objection'.[33]

To highlight the worry of mistaken endorsement, Wilkinson gives the example of a religious person, let's call him John, who spends his time as part of a church congregation, worshipping and fundraising for a preacher who he finds to be enigmatic and trustworthy. However, in reality the preacher is fraudulent – he does not believe in the message he preaches and uses the money raised to fund an extravagant and self-indulgent lifestyle. Wilkinson claims that there has to be an objective and endorsement-independent fact of the matter with regards to whether or not being a follower of the preacher is part of John's prudential good. In this case, John is mistaken about the facts of the situation because they have been hidden from him. Even though John actually does endorse being a committed follower of the preacher, and considers doing so to be fitting with his deep normative commitments, Wilkinson claims that it is not prudentially good for him because of these hidden facts (Wilkinson: 180).

Consider an alternative example of a subdued and dominated house-husband who is oppressed by his wife (Sumner: 156-170). Under these conditions, the husband accepts his identity as a submissive and abused partner, so does not consider his ill-treatment as conflicting with his deep normative commitments. In fact, due to the manipulation inflicted on him by his wife, the husband endorses this ill-treatment as fitting with his own convictions about what is good for him. In this case, we might think that alienating the husband from his normative convictions would be good for him, because he is fundamentally mistaken about the value of the situation and what constitutes proper treatment. The husband's endorsement does not accurately track what is prudentially good for him.

---

[33] For those who argue for the correctness objection or an objection very similar, see Brandt (1996), Lazenby (2016), Nussbaum (2001), Rosati (1995), Sen (1989), and Sumner (1996).

We can reply to the correctness objection by re-stating that the endorsement constraint is not a full theory of well-being, but is merely a necessary *constraint* on a theory of well-being. This constraint leaves room for the claim that some actions, objects or state of affairs may not have impersonal value, and one's endorsement cannot miraculously transform something that is not impersonally valuable into something that has prudential value. With regards to the example of John, the endorsement constraint leaves space for the claim that in fact following a fraudulent preacher is *not* impersonally valuable, and so one's endorsement of it does not make it a constitutive part of one's well-being. As for the dominated house-husband, we could similarly deny that being manipulated is impersonally valuable, so that the husband's manipulated endorsement of ill-treatment does not make it a constitutive part of his well-being. This means that the endorsement constraint still leaves room for the possibility that one's endorsement does not make something prudentially good if it is directed towards something that has no impersonal value.

3.6.3. The Idealisation Clause

The proponent of the correctness objection, however, might further reply that even if something does have impersonal value, it could still be the case than an agent is mistaken about whether or not it fits with her deeply held normative commitments. The agent might fail to endorse something that she may have endorsed if she was not mistaken, or endorse something that she would not have endorsed if she was not mistaken. To alleviate this worry of mistaken endorsement, I propose that we include a counter-factual idealisation clause as part of the endorsement constraint. This idealisation clause states that talent development is prudentially good for an agent if she would endorse it under idealised conditions that mitigate for mistaken beliefs and judgements. What constitutes these idealised conditions will differ according to how strong or weak we think the condition ought to be.

Strong idealisation conditions have usually been formulated in terms of full-information and full-rationality. For example, Peter Railton's idealisation clause claims that an agent's prudential good consists in what he would pursue were he "to contemplate his present situation from a standpoint fully and vividly informed about himself and his circumstances, and entirely free of cognitive error or lapses of instrumental rationality" (Railton 2003: 14). Robert Firth similarly claims that the ideal agent is "omniscient, omnipercipient, disinterested, dispassionate, consistent, and normal in other respects" (Firth 1952, cited in Enoch: 759, see also Rosati 1995: 297). What these strong idealisation accounts have in common is the fact that under ideal conditions, an agent will be fully informed about the facts of the situation, and will be fully rational so as to avoid cognitive error when making decisions about what is valuable to her.

These strong accounts face two objections, the first raises a cognitive issue, and the second, a motivational concerns. First, it seems impossible that a person will ever be fully informed or rational in the way that is prescribed (Sobel 1994: 784-810). A fully ideal person would have to be able to receive and understand all the various points of view that come with different states of affairs and experiences, and at the same time have the capacity to retain the information gathered from this in order to make effective decisions about what the actual agent ought to endorse. As Rosati has argued, for an agent to have these capacities she would need to be super-human, and this means that knowledge about an agent's well-being will only be accessible to those who possess these super-human capacities. This is problematic because it is highly unlikely, if not impossible, that any human could ever attain such idealised capacities or be in an epistemic position to access the information that is accumulated whilst under these idealised conditions (Rosati 1995: 299, 315-317).[34]

Second, if the ideal agent is one that is fully informed and fully rational, it seems as if that agent will be far removed in cognitive abilities and life experience from the actual agent whose well-being we are considering (Rosati 1995: 311;

---

[34] Rosati gives a long and detailed list of the super-human qualities that this strongly ideal agent must possess: "At a minimum, she would have to have capacities of reason, memory, and imagination far surpassing those she actually has. She would have to be able to have all the necessary experiences and keep them clearly before her mind, remembering them as experienced in themselves and as experienced in relation to what comes before and after. In addition, she would have to retain features of her personality that enable her to experience her lives as she would as the persons living them, desiring and being motivated as he would be from within those lives, while losing all features of her personality that keep her from absorbing information" (Rosati 1995: 310).

Railton 2003: 21). As a result, what the ideal agent would endorse may be very different from what the actual agent would endorse. This means that the actual agent will find it difficult to accept and endorse that which the ideal agent claims to be prudentially good for her (Lazenby: 196). In this way, even if we do include the idealisation clause into the endorsement constraint, the actual agent may still be alienated from what is considered to constitute her well-being, and this was the exact problem that the endorsement constraint was trying to avoid.[35]

Given these two objections, the counterfactual idealisation clause that is to be incorporated into the endorsement constraint should not appeal to an agent being *fully* informed and *fully* rational. Instead, I propose that the agent should be under 'optimal' conditions, such that she is *optimally* informed and *optimally* rational. These conditions are ones that enable an actual agent to make an optimal decision about what is valuable to her and what fits with her deeply held normative commitments, as she is now. In order to be under these optimal conditions, the agent does not need to undergo drastic changes to her cognitive abilities, nor does she need to experience every point of view that comes with a potential way of life. Instead, the agent merely needs to be in conducive epistemic and cognitive conditions that are optimal for making good decisions and critically reflecting on her life as it is now. Rosati claims that these conditions are "whatever normally attainable conditions we ordinarily regard optimal for reflecting on judgements and making decisions about our own good. Such conditions include that a person is paying attention, that she be free from emotional distress or neurotic worries, and that she not be over-looking readily available information" (Rosati 1995: 300, 324; see also Dorsey 2012: 1).

There may be a danger that the way in which these optimal conditions are specified will be *ad hoc* and collapse into the kinds of fully idealised conditions that have just been argued against (Enoch: 766-769). As such, there needs to be a principled reason for why we limit what counts as improved counterfactual conditions to be optimal, rather than fully idealised. Given the objections to the full idealisation conditions described above, the desiderata for such a limit must be that (a) the counter-factual conditions are not impossible to attain, and (b) the

---

[35] On this objection see also Tiffany (2003) and Sobel (2001, 2009).

actual agent is not alienated from what her counterfactual self would endorse. Therefore, I propose that the counterfactual conditions in question are no longer 'optimal' but worryingly fully ideal, at the point at which we cease to regard the agent as the same agent as she is now; this would be when the counterfactual agent and the actual agent no longer hold the same deep normative commitments that shape who they are and determine their conception of the good life. [36]

For example, when making a decision about whether I ought to develop my talent for playing the clarinet, I would not be expected to be fully informed about each alternative and the kind of person I would be when pursuing these alternatives, nor would I be expected to be completely rational, avoiding all bias or cognitive error; being fully idealised in this way would alter who I am. Instead, I will only be expected to be as informed and rational as I can be in order to make an optimal decision about whether developing my talent will fit with my deep normative commitments, as they are now. There is no reason why I need to be fully idealised to make this kind of optimal decision.

It could be argued that without perfectly idealised epistemic and cognitive capacities, an agent will lack critical information or evaluative capacities that are necessary to judge whether a state of affairs or object does indeed fit with her deeply held normative commitments. However, an agent who is under optimal decision-making conditions and who cares about her well-being will be inclined to make as informed and rational a decision as possible. As a result, even if the agent does initially lack important information, being under optimal decision-making conditions will require that she compensates for this lack just enough to make a

---

[36] There may be further worries about this specification of optimal conditions and the way in which they differ from fully idealised conditions. For example, it is not clear where the limit that I have specified will lie, and if it is possible to ever locate such a limit; this is because every new piece of information or change in cognitive abilities, even if they are small changes necessary for making good and optimal decisions, may potentially have an impact on an agent's character and her deeply held normative commitments. The limit that I specify also requires an agent's identity to be stable enough such that we can judge an agent to be the 'same' agent at different points in time. For sake of argument in this chapter, I accept that there is a burden of proof to specify what these optimal conditions are in such a way that is not vague or problematically *ad hoc*. Given the fact that *fully* idealised conditions are implausible in the way I have specified in this chapter, this is a burden I am willing to accept for sake of argument.

good decision about her well-being, either by educating herself further or by referring to expert testimony (Rosati 2006: 61, 43-44). Similarly, if an agent lacks important cognitive capacities, being under optimal decision-making conditions will require an agent to remedy for this in some way, for example, by not making decisions under the influence of drugs or alcohol, or ensuring that one's decisions are as logically coherent as possible.

Importantly, these optimal conditions will be procedural, and not normatively laden with substantial claims about what is good for an agent, such that what counts as an 'optimal' condition for decision-making is that which makes an agent arrive at a particular answer about what she endorses. If this were the case, then we could sneak in our favoured objective theory of well-being, perfectionism for example, claiming that optimal decision-making conditions are those in which an agent just agrees with the commitments of perfectionism. Instead, what counts as an optimal condition can be determined quite independently from the reasons that we give for supporting a particular theory of well-being. For example, as already highlighted, Colburn and Rosati justify an appeal to optimal conditions with regards to the value of autonomy, and Dworkin, with regards to authenticity.

I argue that the procedural optimisation clause is all that is needed to alleviate the worry of mistaken endorsement and alienation. This becomes clear when referring back to the examples of John the duped religious person and the subdued house-husband. The reason why we worried about those instances of mistaken and manipulated endorsement was not because the agents did not reach the *right* decision about what to endorse. This would just be to beg the question in favour of the objectivist, assuming that there is an account of what is good for a person independent of their endorsement. Instead, we worried about the mistaken and manipulated endorsement because of the way in which the agents made their decisions – the fact that they were in sub-optimal conditions and subject to cognitive impairment, and in the way in which this violated the values of integrity, authenticity and autonomy. These sub-optimal decision-making conditions are not conducive for making decisions about what is of value in one's life. To be in the conditions that are conducive for making decisions about what is valuable, an agent does not need to be *fully* informed or rational. Instead, the agent only needs to be *optimally* informed and rational in a way that arrives at conditions conducive to making decisions about what is valuable in her life, as she is now. Therefore, the inclusion of optimal conditions is not *ad hoc*, but is necessary for the practice of good decision-making.

The endorsement constraint can now be restated to accommodate for the correctness objection, by including an idealisation clause that specifies optimal decision-making conditions rather than fully ideal conditions:

> *Endorsement Constraint**. Talent Development *T* is prudentially good for an agent *A* if and only if *A* endorses (or would endorse if under optimal decision-making conditions) the internal and external normative commitments that are necessarily required to bring about *T*, as part of or complimentary to *A*'s deeply held normative commitments.

I will now go on to discuss and respond to three objections that can be raised against this formulation of the endorsement constraint.

3.6.4. Three Further Objections

Objection One. It could be argued that acceptance of the endorsement constraint results in there being no fact of the matter about whether talent development is prudentially good for those who are unable to engage in the required optimal decision-making process. For example, children or those with cognitive impairments may be unable to arrive at an optimal decision about whether developing their talents fits with their deep normative commitments, and consequently, they will be unable to make judgements about their prudential good.

This objection can be responded to by highlighting that the endorsement constraint's idealisation condition is counter-factual. It does not state that the agent must *actually* be under optimal conditions, but only states that talent development is prudentially good for the agent *if they would* endorse it under optimal conditions. For an agent who is unable to form optimal decisions, it is her counterfactual endorsement that counts as a necessary constraint when determining whether talent development is prudentially good for her. What makes talent development good for an agent is whether they *would* endorse it if they were in such a position to be able to do so.

Objection Two. Wilkinson argues that the endorsement constraint is implausible because it implies that when an agent changes her mind about whether she endorses a state of affairs, then the prudential value of that state of affairs will also change accordingly. This is problematic because it means that a change of mind on one's deathbed, for example, will drastically alter the value of one's life. This is an unattractive consequence of the endorsement constraint, as it seems that one's level of well-being could rest ultimately on one final change of mind irrespective of the positive value that one has accumulated throughout one's life (Wilkinson: 184, 188).

In response, it is not evident why it should be problematic that an agent changes her mind about whether she endorses the development of her talent. This is clear when considering the reasons why this change of mind might occur. First, it might be that an agent was not actually in optimal decision-making conditions when originally endorsing the development of her talent. This means that in fact her endorsement did not conform to the conditions set out by the endorsement constraint, and so developing her talent was not actually a constitutive part of her well-being. If the agent subsequently changes her mind under optimal decision-making conditions, her lack of endorsement will not have drastically altered the prudential value of that agent's talent development in the way that Wilkinson suggests.

Second, it could be that the agent decides that the commitments that come with the development of her talent no longer fit with her deeply held normative commitments. Either the agent's deep normative commitments will have changed over time, or there will have been a change in the internal or external commitments that are necessary to bring about the development of her talent. For example, it might be that given the developments of a particular sport, the agent will have to change her body shape or strength requirements over time and in a way that changes the type of normative commitments that come with the development of her skill for that sport. If the agent changes her mind about what she endorses as a result of these changes, she is merely re-evaluating the fit between the development of her talent and her deep normative commitments. As such, changes of mind are not a problem for those who accept the endorsement constraint. As long as the re-evaluation occurs under optimal decision-making conditions, the agent can consistently endorse the development of her talent at an earlier time, but not endorse the development of that same talent at a later time. This also means that whether or not developing one's talent is a constitutive part of one's well-being will depend on and alter according to this re-evaluation of endorsement.

It is not clear why this re-evaluation of one's endorsement really is problematic in the way that Wilkinson describes. Accepting the endorsement constraint *does* entail that there is no objective and context-independent fact of the matter about whether developing one's talents is prudentially good. And this means that whether or not talent development is a constitutive part of an agent's well-being will depend on that agent's endorsement at different times. We would only object to the plausibility of this claim if we already assumed or held a purely objective account of well-being, claiming that there is a context-independent and response-independent fact of the matter about whether talent development is prudentially good. Yet given the arguments that I have offered in this chapter, there is good reason to reject pure objectivist accounts of well-being, insofar as they are unable to avoid the alienation problem. At the very least, we have to hold a hybrid view that accommodates an agent's endorsement as a necessary constraint on what counts as prudentially good for that agent. This means that the objection raised by Wilkinson about the implausibility of changes of mind is only problematic for my account of the endorsement constraint if we beg the question in favour of objectivism about well-being.[37] Furthermore, it is not the case that accepting the endorsement constraint as a constraint on theories of well-being amounts to the claim that whether or not one's life was, overall, a good life depends *sufficiently* on one's endorsement of that life. The endorsement

[37] It might also be the case that a response-independent account merely requires some kind of inter-subjectively acknowledged standard and this need not take the objectivist form. And so, the objection is only a problem if we beg the question, more generally in favour of response-independent theories of well-being, more generally defined. Thanks to Glen Pettigrove for highlighting this point.

constraint is merely a *necessary* constraint, and as mentioned above, the goodness of one's life, or the truth about what constitutes one's well-being, will also rely on other necessary conditions, such as the *value* of the pursuit in question.[38]

Objection Three. Wilkinson further argues that the endorsement constraint does not specify at what stage during the development of an agent's talent her endorsement should count as determining whether her talent development is prudentially good. He claims that this detail is left unspecified because once it has been determined, it highlights that the endorsement constraint is implausible (Wilkinson: 181-188).

Wilkinson argues that 'later endorsement', endorsement that occurs *after* the development of the talent, is the most plausible candidate to be included into the endorsement constraint (Wilkinson: 182-183). This is because later endorsement offers a more privileged epistemological and phenomenological position from which to make judgements about the value of one's talent development and whether that development fits with one's deep normative commitments. As Wilkinson claims, later endorsement "is made in the light of a genuine engagement with an activity, whereas the earlier endorsement expresses a conviction not based on personal experience" (Wilkinson: 187; see also Dworkin 2000: 269).

However, if later endorsement really is what matters, then the endorsement constraint faces two problems which show that it is implausible. First, what the agent would later endorse may in fact be far removed from what the agent would endorse as she is now. In that case, the endorsement constraint

---

[38] Wilkinson suggests that in order to respond to the changes of mind objection, one should claim that "the longer something is endorsed for, the greater the contribution to well-being" (Wilkinson: 184). However, there is no indication that the length of endorsement has any substantial part to play in determining whether the endorsement is carried out under optimal decision-making conditions or really does represent a consideration of the agent's deep normative commitments. And so, the length of time for which an agent endorses something does not determine whether talent development is constitutive of an agent's well-being, and Wilkinson himself quickly rejects this as a plausible response for those who advocate the endorsement constraint. His conclusion, however, is that this is the only response and seeing as it is unsuccessful, the endorsement constraint is implausible as a result.

would not really be a solution to the alienation problem; what the agent later endorses may be alienating for the agent as she is prior to or during the development of her talent. Second, when making decisions about what we ought to do in order to live a life full of prudential goodness, we need to be able to determine whether a state of affairs is prudentially good *before* an agent engages with it and potentially subjects herself to something that may be bad for her and significantly reduces her level of well-being. Relying on later endorsement does not allow us to determine these important practical questions about whether or not an agent ought to develop her talents.

We can respond to this objection by simply denying that later endorsement is indeed the kind of endorsement that ought to be included into the endorsement constraint. Wilkinson's choice of later endorsement as being the most plausible relies on the assumption that we cannot assign a significant value to a future experience without a subjective experience of it. Although an agent's endorsement before and during the development of her talent may be lacking in extensive personal experience of the development itself, there is nothing to say that this subjective experience is the only or most privileged way of making decisions about what we ought to do or what we ought to endorse. There are other ways to assign values to experiences without this subjective privilege.

For example, Ruth Chang suggests that an all-things-considered endorsement need not rely on a full subjective experience of what is being endorsed. We can tell what a future action or state of affairs might be like by referring to other similar subjective experiences, reliable testimony from experts or those who know us well, as well as appealing to traditional rational choice theory that will give us the tools to assign predictive value to future outcomes based on probabilities (Chang 2015: 247-249, 253). This means that even though an agent may not have a full experience of what the development of her talent will involve, it is still possible that she is able to make a considered and rational judgement about whether the commitments that come with the development of her talent will fit with her deeply held normative commitments. For the agent to be in optimal decision-making conditions, we only need to state that she has enough information to make an informed decision about what is prudentially good for her. And this account of optimal-information does not necessarily need to include a full subjective account of the epistemological and phenomenological experience of the development of one's talents.

Therefore, the endorsement constraint *does* specify at what stage one's endorsement should count as determining whether the development of one's talent is prudentially good. The constraint prescribes that one's endorsement counts when made under optimal decision-making conditions, and this could conceivably occur at *any* stage of one's talent development. This means that the endorsement constraint is not guilty of being implausible in the way that Wilkinson suggests; there is no problem of alienation, and an agent can make decisions about whether or not her talent development is prudentially good for her *before* fully engaging in that development.[39]

I have now responded to three of the most incriminating objections that could be raised against my formulation of the endorsement constraint, and it is plausible to conclude that for the development of an agent's talent to count as prudentially good, that agent must endorse the development of her talent. This appeal to endorsement is a necessary constraint on all theories of well-being and is stated as follows:

---

[39] There may be cases in which an agent is unsure about whether the development of her talent fits with her deep normative commitments. How does this impact the plausibility of the endorsement constraint? First, in situations of uncertainty about endorsement we could ask whether the agent really is under optimal conditions – she may not have all the relevant facts or the optimal cognitive abilities to reflect clearly and rationally. In this case, to determine whether developing her talents is good for her, we would consider whether the agent would endorse it if under optimal conditions. The apparent uncertainty is merely an instance of an agent not being under the right kind of decision-making conditions. Second, it might be that the agent is in fact under optimal decision-making conditions, but nevertheless is still unsure and unable to make a decision about whether she endorses the development of her talent. As Chang suggests, this means that the normative significance of the reasons both in favour of and against developing her talent are *equal* or *on par* (Chang 2002). What the agent should choose in these circumstances is a question for rational choice theory. For example, Chang's theory of hybrid voluntarism claims that we should simply 'plump' for one of the normatively equal options (Chang 2004; Chang 2013; Chang 2015). When it comes to assessing the plausibility of the endorsement constraint, however, we need only admit that once such a decision has been made, then that decision of endorsement – or lack thereof – determines whether developing one's talents is prudentially good.

Endorsement Constraint*. Talent development *T* is prudentially good for an agent *A* if and only if *A* endorses (or would endorse if under optimal decision-making conditions) the normative commitments that are necessarily required to bring about *T*, as part of or complimentary to *A's* deeply held normative commitments.

3.7. Conclusion

Given that the endorsement constraint is a necessary condition for determining what constitutes an agent's well-being, this means that the monist perfectionist's claim, that developing one's talents is objectively prudentially good, is implausible. The welfare perfectionist makes the claim that developing one's talents is objectively prudentially good. However, this claim is subject to the worry of alienation, which highlights that the agent will potentially be alienated if the internal and external commitments that come with development of her talent do not fit with her own deep normative commitments. To avoid this lack of fit, I argued that we ought to adopt the endorsement constraint as part of a hybrid perfectionist account, which states that talent development is only prudentially good for an agent if and only if she endorses (or would endorse if under optimal decision-making conditions) the normative commitments that are necessarily required to bring about the development of her talent, as part of or complimentary to her deeply held normative commitments.

The counterfactual idealisation clause was added to accommodate the correctness objection, that alienation is in fact not intrinsically bad, for example when an agent makes a mistake with regards to what she endorses. The idealisation clause that I argue for prescribes only optimal rather than ideal conditions for decision-making about one's well-being, and makes no substantive normative claims about what an agent *ought* to endorse.

It is important to remember that the endorsement constraint is only a necessary feature of an account of well-being, not a sufficient one. This means that perfectionism could quite plausibly accommodate the endorsement constraint and still hold that there are some goods that are objectively valuable *simpliciter*. This kind of perfectionism would be a hybrid account, stating that in order for an object or state of affairs with positive objective value to be considered as prudentially good *for* an agent, that object or state of affairs also has to be endorsed by that agent. This allows the perfectionist to maintain that the endorsement of the agent does not by itself *make* something prudentially good, but only together with what already has perfectionist value. Consequently, endorsement cannot make prudentially good something that has no perfectionist value.

However, for this hybrid perfectionism to be plausible, the perfectionist also has to be able to prove that talent development does indeed have positive perfectionist value. Earlier in this chapter I also objected to both moral and welfare perfectionism precisely on these grounds. I argued for the 'excellence objection', which stated that perfectionism cannot generate the priority of developing specifically our talents over any other competency that we may have. This is because developing one's talent may not in fact excellently and fully perfect one's essential human capacities, and furthermore, the goodness of developing a particular talent is conditional on whether the particular skill in question is already deemed valuable or morally permissible. Therefore, even if perfectionists accept a hybrid account that incorporates endorsement *and* objective perfectionist value of certain goods and states of affairs, they are unable to claim that developing one's talent is indeed an objective perfectionist value in this way.

As a result, moral perfectionism cannot successfully claim that developing one's talents is objectively good and so morally required of us. This means that the moral duty to develop one's talents is only *prima facie*, as it cannot be derived successfully from the claims made by moral perfectionism. Similarly, when it comes to one's prudential good, welfare perfection cannot successfully claim that developing one's talent is an objective *pro tanto* prudential good, insofar as welfare perfectionism cannot successfully derive those reasons from its commitments.

This is not to say that a *pro tanto* prudential reason to develop one's talent and a *pro tanto* moral duty to develop one's talent cannot be derived from any theory of well-being or morality. It may be that there are theories that are able to respond to the objections that I have raised in both this and the previous chapter, and can thus successfully argue for a *pro tanto* duty or reason to develop one's talents. In this chapter I have argued that with regards to well-being, however, whether or not there is a *pro tanto* prudential reason to develop one's talents will always be conditional on accommodating the endorsement constraint. In the next chapter I argue that with regards to morality, whether or not there is a *pro tanto* moral duty to develop one's talents will also be conditional on meeting the endorsement constraint.

Chapter Four

Moral Demandingness and Talent Development

4.1. Introduction

Both Kant and moral perfectionists explicitly claim that there is a moral obligation to develop one's talents. In the previous two chapters I have explained why we ought to reject the arguments that these theories give in support of their claims that there is a strong connection between talent development and morality. This does not mean, however, that a moral obligation to develop one's talents can never be formulated by a moral theory. Even though other moral theories may not explicitly argue for the necessary connection between morality and talent development, nor claim that the moral obligation to develop one's talents is a fundamental commitment of the theory itself, it still might be the case that a moral theory will demand that an agent develops her talents. Such a demand would arise either because failing to develop one's talents results in acting against the particular principles of the moral theory, or that developing one's talents will promote adherence to the principles of the moral theory. For example, whether or not consequentialism requires an agent to develop her talents will depend on the various calculations that determine what consequentialism requires – that is, if doing so would promote, over-all, the best state of affairs (see Hurley 2009: 1; Scanlon: 81). To give another example, care ethics, would presumably require one to develop one's talents if failing to do so undermines the guiding principle that "we act rightly or permissibly if our actions express or exhibit an attitude/motive of caring toward others" (Slote 2007: 10).

There are two ways we can assess a moral theory's demand that one ought to develop one's talents. First, we can reject the idea that the theory, properly understood, *does* generate the moral obligation to develop one's talents. For example, we might question whether the consequentialist calculation really does imply that one ought to develop one's talents, or in the case of care ethics, that doing so really does promote a caring attitude towards others. This was the strategy that I adopted in the previous two chapters of this dissertation; I argued that the commitments of both perfectionism and Kant's moral theory do not successfully give rise to a moral duty to develop one's talents. I focussed particularly on these two theories because of their explicit claims that we do indeed have such an obligation.

The second way to assess the plausibility of the moral demand to develop one's talents does not require an analysis of the commitments of each particular theory. Even if a moral theory can derive an obligation to develop one's talents from its commitments and principles, we can still object to the obligation by referring to external reasons that can be raised, irrespective of the specific features of each moral theory.

It is this second strategy that I adopt in this chapter by appealing to a particular form of the demandingness objection. More generally, the demandingness objection states that if a moral theory requires of one to unreasonably sacrifice one's non-moral commitments, then that moral theory and its moral demands are implausibly demanding: we ought to reject an account of morality that prescribes over-demanding obligations. Specifically in relation to talent development, I argue that irrespective of how a particular moral theory formulates its claim that we have a moral obligation to develop our talents, this obligation has the potential to be unreasonably demanding because an agent will be required to unreasonably sacrifice her non-moral commitments. If this is the case, then the obligation can be overridden by one's non-moral concerns, and the moral obligation to develop one's talents can be classed as overly demanding. As such, I specify a negative condition on any moral theory that claims one has a moral obligation to develop one's talents, namely, that talent development cannot be overly demanding. This condition holds no matter which moral theory one adopts.

In what follows, I argue that the demandingness objection that is relevant to the moral obligation to develop one's talents should be understood in terms of the endorsement constraint that I presented in the previous chapter. I claim that the obligation to develop one's talent is only reasonably demanding insofar as an agent endorses the normative commitments that are necessary for bringing about the development of her talent. If one does have a *pro tanto* obligation to develop one's talent, it will thus be conditional on one's endorsement of that development; lack of this endorsement rules that the moral obligation to develop one's talents is too demanding.

To argue for this claim, I need to explain and defend an account of what over-demandingness is when it comes to the moral obligation to develop one's talents. I begin by stating the demandingness objection in its most general form, before considering two specific versions – the objection from overridingness, and the content-based objection. In Section Three I argue that we should not understand over-demandingness in terms of overridingness, and in Section Four I argue for my own content-based interpretation of the demandingness objection, appealing to the endorsement constraint. In Section Five I respond to three objections that can be raised against my formulation of the demandingness objection, and in Section Six I conclude by highlighting the implications that my account of demandingness raises for the relationship between morality and talent development.

4.2. The Demandingness Objection

The most general formulation of the demandingness objection is stated as follows: a particular moral theory or moral requirement is overly demanding if it asks of an agent to unreasonably sacrifice her non-moral commitments. If morality is over-demanding, it will require us to do things that we have good reason to think should not be demanded of us. Any moral theory that claims we have these requirements is mistaken, because they are in fact not actually required – something has gone wrong with the commitments of a theory that claims we ought to do something that we are not in fact required to do.

There are three initial qualifications to make regarding this statement of the demandingness objection. First, my focus in this chapter is not on the demandingness of morality more generally, or a specific moral theory, but with the particular moral requirement to develop one's talents. This means that any moral theory that claims we have a moral obligation to develop our talents is potentially subject to the demandingness objection that I propose. From this it follows that I am not concerned with cases where developing one's talents is merely seen as morally *permissible*, such that a moral theory merely *allows* us to develop our talents. Instead, the particular case that I focus on in this chapter is the plausibility of when morality specifically *requires* of us that we ought to develop our talents.

Second, it is important to qualify that whether or not a moral requirement is unreasonably demanding will be determined by the demands that morality makes on our *non-moral* commitments, not our moral ones. This is because the demandingness objection assumes, for the sake of argument, that if a moral theory claims we have a moral obligation to do *X*, then doing *X* will be consistent with the other commitments of that moral theory (Goodin: 2). I take it for granted, therefore, that if a theory prescribes that there is a moral obligation to develop one's talents, then that obligation does not problematically conflict with any other moral obligation that is prescribed by that same theory. Given that, the demandingness objection claims that the moral requirement to develop one's talents is too *non-morally* demanding, implausibly conflicting with our own personal commitments.

Finally, the focus of this chapter is not merely whether the moral obligation to develop one's talents counts as demanding *simpliciter*. The very nature of talent development often results in the fact that doing so will be somewhat demanding; developing one's skills for a musical instrument or training to be an athlete, for example, can be extremely strenuous and challenging tasks. However, we do not necessarily judge this demandingness to be unjustified or problematic, but a reasonable part of what it is to develop one's talents. That morality requires this reasonable demandingness is not the point of contention here; instead, the demandingness objection I propose focuses on the extent to which the moral obligation to develop one's talents counts as *unreasonably* or *overly* demanding.

Given these qualifications, the demandingness objection that I will be discussing in this chapter can be stated more accurately as follows: the particular moral obligation to develop one's talents is overly demanding if it asks of an agent to unreasonably sacrifice her non-moral commitments. In order to assess the plausibility of this demandingness objection, it is necessary to understand the way in which the moral obligation to develop one's talents could be considered as overly demanding.

First, it could be argued that the moral obligation to develop one's talents is over demanding due to morality's 'overridingness' over non-moral concerns. The claim is that once we have decided what counts as a moral obligation given by the commitments of a particular moral theory, morality is then deemed to be authoritative over one's other non-moral concerns, and prescribes what we have *most* reason to do (Scheffler 1992: 52-71; Van Ackeren & Sticker: 78). This means that in order to fulfil one's moral duty, one is expected to give up various deeply held and significant personal commitments. As a result of this overridingness, morality is seen to be unreasonably over-demanding. In the next section, I will argue that in fact this interpretation of the demandingness objection does not capture the reasons why the moral obligation to develop one's talents may be considered as over-demanding. This is because the moral obligation may still be unreasonably demanding even when the worry of morality's purported overridingness over non-moral concerns has been responded to.

Instead, I argue that the demandingness objection, when focussed on the moral obligation to develop one's talents, should be interpreted as a claim about the substantive values and commitments that come with the particular content of the moral demand itself (Scheffler 1992: 98-109; Van Ackeren & Sticker: 78). I claim that the moral demand to develop one's talents is over-demanding insofar as the commitments required to comply with the obligation asks an agent to unreasonably neglect her non-moral commitments. In Section Four, I will argue that what counts as an unreasonable neglect of one's non-moral commitments is grounded in a failure to meet the endorsement constraint, such that an agent does not endorse the normative commitments that are necessary to bring about the development of her talent as fitting with her own deeply held personal concerns.

For now, however, I will go on to argue that we ought to reject the interpretation of the demandingness objection as grounded in morality's overridingness. [40]

4.3. Demandingness and Overridingness

The requirements of morality are often considered to be over-demanding in virtue of the fact that they are able to override all other non-moral concerns. This is to say, morality is rationally authoritative when deciding what we have an all-things-considered reason to do. The idea that morality is normative and gives us reasons for what we ought to do is not what is in contention here; instead, it is the claim that morality gives us a "definitive and decisive" reason, an authoritative reason to perform what is morally required (Dorsey 2012: 6). This rational authority may be problematic, however, in cases where we consider our non-moral concerns to be at least equally as weighty as our moral concerns. It would be wrong, therefore, to allow morality to override these weighty non-moral concerns, neglecting or ignoring significant non-moral concerns when determining what we should do, all-things-considered.

The claim that morality should override all other non-moral concerns in this way is most explicitly argued for in some Kantian accounts of morality. Kant argues that morality should always have authority over our non-moral concerns – if morality requires us to do something then this is what we *must* do, even if it conflicts with other non-moral commitments that we may have. As such, one's non-moral reasons lose their rational force when deciding what we ought to do (Walla: 737; Van Ackeren & Sticker: 84, 81). Because Kant's position here considers morality to be rationality authoritative over one's non-moral concerns, let's call this position a version of 'strong moral rationalism'.

---

[40] Scheffler differentiates two further types of demandingness objection – the objection from *scope* and a *procedural* objection. However, for the purposes of this chapter, I assume that both the scope and procedural objections can be accommodated by the two versions of demandingness that I discuss – the overridingness and content-based objections (see Scheffler 1992: 18-51; Van Ackeren & Sticker: 7, 78).

However, we need not adopt such a strong claim in order to maintain that morality is overriding. Instead of asserting that all non-moral concerns lose their normative force in the face of moral reasons, we could accept that some non-moral concerns retain their normative pull when deciding what we ought to do. This weaker claim allows the moral rationalist to explain why one often feels sadness or regret when one neglects one's non-moral commitments. Even so, 'weak moral rationalism' will still advocate the position that morality is able to outweigh these normatively weighty non-moral concerns when deciding what we ought to do all-things-considered.

This weaker form of moral rationalism is still subject to the worry that it may result in an over-demanding conception of what morality requires from moral agents. The concern is that there are often times in which our non-moral concerns *do* give us normatively strong reasons for action, such that our moral reasons do not seem normatively powerful enough to be legitimately authoritative (Sobel 2007: 14). In these circumstances, where our normatively weighty non-moral considerations conflict with what is morally required of us, we might think that what morality demands of us is unreasonable, as it will automatically override the significant normative weight of our own personal commitments.

There are, however, some cases in which there seem to be good reasons why the requirements of morality ought to normatively outweigh our non-moral concerns. For example, we might think that a personal desire to enjoy a beer with friends or to buy the latest Taylor Swift album should not dictate what we ought to do all things considered, nor should those commitments legitimately trump what morality requires us to do. It is not the case that the demandingness objection claims that our moral obligation to help those in need should always be trumped by a personal desire to indulge in my desire to grow my music library. Because of this, when we worry about morality overriding one's non-moral concerns, those concerns relate to the personal commitments that have significant value for one's life and bestow it with meaning. These are the types of commitments that in Chapter Three I termed 'deep normative commitments' – they are constitutive of our conception of the good life and sense of self, and as such give us reasons for choosing and acting in a particular way (see again Bagnoli: 5; Moseley: 60; Rivera: 71; Scheffler 1992: 123).

The demandingness objection, when it is understood in terms of overridingness, is therefore concerned with instances of when one's deeply held normative commitments are outweighed by moral requirements due to the fact that morality is considered to be rationally authoritative. This is argued to be problematic because sacrificing these deep normative commitments can be unreasonably costly – these commitments are extremely valuable to us, they give our lives meaning, as well as shape our character and conception of who we are. Therefore, in some cases at least, due to morality's overridingness, what morality requires will demand that one neglects one's own character and sense of self.

Having explained the demandingness objection understood in terms of overridingness, I will now argue that this formulation of the objection does not capture the reasons why the moral obligation to develop one's talents ought to be considered as over-demanding. This is because it is conceptually possible that talent development can be implausibly demanding in ways that the overridingness objection does not accommodate for. This is shown by the fact that even when the worry of morality's purported overridingness over non-moral concerns has been responded to, such that morality is no longer considered to be over-demanding, the moral obligation to develop one's talents can still be determined as over-demanding. That is, even if we have responded successfully to the overridingness objection, there is still a problem of over-demandingness, and as such, over-demandingness should not be understood in terms of overridingness. In order to argue for this claim, I will now discuss the two ways in which we can respond to the worry of overridingness, and show that no matter which of the two responses is taken, we can still argue that the moral obligation to develop one's talents could be over-demanding. Both responses or strategies still leave conceptual space for talent development to be over-demanding, and so there must be reasons to think that talent development is overly demanding that is not comprehensively captured by the overridingness version of the demandingness objection.

First Response. To ensure that moral requirements are not too demanding for an agent, some moral rationalists keep their commitment to morality's overridingness over non-moral concerns, but adjust the content of morality so that significant non-moral concerns are incorporated into the moral sphere. This means that what counts as a moral concern includes these normatively weighty personal commitments that the demandingness objection claimed to be too costly to outweigh; these deeply held commitments are now classed as *moral* commitments (Sobel 2007: 14). In this way, these non-moral concerns are thought to genuinely belong in the moral sphere and as a result, whether or not the moral obligation to develop our talents is considered to be too demanding will be determined by weighing up all the moral reasons that count for or against doing so; these moral reasons will include the deeply held personal commitments that were originally considered to be non-moral. In this way, the moral rationalist still accepts that morality is overriding, but claims that there is no longer a worry of morality unreasonably demanding of an agent to neglect her deeply held personal commitments.

Samuel Scheffler makes such a move, claiming that even though morality is rationally authoritative, it ought to make room for our non-moral concerns by accommodating them as part of the moral outlook (Scheffler 1992: 122-123; Scheffler 1994: 41-78; see also Berkey: 3026-3029; Dorsey 2012: 17). Other consequentialists have similarly opted to include agent-relative concerns in their conception of morality, so that what morality requires of us is just what we have most reason to do in pursuit of one overarching value – Peter Railton calls this value 'The Good' (Railton 1984; see also Portmore 2012). Railton claims that "it becomes artificial to impose a dichotomy between what is done for the self and what is done for the other. We cannot decompose such relationship into a vector of self-concern and a vector of other-concern" (Railton 1984: 166). In this way, morality would not be subject to the demandingness objection due to the fact that what morality requires *does not* demand an agent to unreasonably sacrifice her deeply held personal commitments. These personal commitments are instead incorporated into morality.[41]

---

[41] Ruth Chang has argued for her own account of this overarching value, in which both moral concerns and non-moral concerns figure as constituent parts of the decision-making process about what we ought to do all-things-considered. When determining the right balance between morality and prudence, Chang claims that we appeal to a more comprehensive value that she considers to be 'nameless'; however, just because we do not have a name for this comprehensive value this does not mean that our appeal to it is any less warranted (Chang 2004).

Adopting this first strategy, however, does not help to determine whether a moral obligation, such as the obligation to develop one's talents, counts as 'overly' demanding. In fact, we can still claim that an obligation is overly-demanding even if we do incorporate our personal commitments into the moral sphere. This is because the kind of move that Railton and Scheffler make only shifts the deliberation about demandingness into the moral sphere; within this sphere however, we would still need to determine whether or not our deep normative commitments unreasonably conflict with other moral concerns. If one's personal commitments were in fact included within the sphere of morality, in order to determine whether an obligation was overly demanding we would now weigh up the competing *moral* concerns, and consider whether they are normatively weighty enough to override the obligation.

Merely re-labelling our personal concerns as 'moral' does not help locate the potential demandingness of a moral requirement – we are still left asking whether one moral requirement conflicts with another moral requirement, and whether that conflict counts as unreasonable. Consequently, this first strategy at resolving the worry of overridingness does not provide a plausible way to resolve the worry of overdemandingness. This is because we are still left with the question of how to determine whether one's moral concerns will unreasonably demand too much of us with regards to another moral concern. As such, there may still be reasons why the moral obligation to develop one's talents counts as over-demanding that the overridingness objection does not capture.[42]

Second Response. The second way to ensure that moral requirements are not too demanding in terms of overridingness is just to reject altogether the notion that morality is overriding, and claim that morality need not be authoritative over

---

[42] Bernard Williams rejects the strategy of incorporating our non-moral concerns into the moral sphere, because he claims that this will force us to make decisions about our own well-being in the same impartial and impersonal way that we do when making moral decisions. This is problematic, Williams claims, because this type of impartial decision-making alienates an agent from her own sense of self and her deep normative commitments (Williams 2006: 20, 31; Dorsey 2012: 6). For sake of argument I leave Williams' impartiality objection aside here. For a response to the objection see Fairbanks and Dorsey, who both argue that the objection fails to distinguish between second-order and first-order impartiality (Fairbanks: 6; Dorsey 2102: 19).

our non-moral concerns when deciding what we have an all-things-considered reason to do. As such, our non-moral considerations will be able to trump our moral concerns when they are significantly normatively weighty. By rejecting morality's rational authority over non-moral concerns we do not need to adjust the content of morality, but instead admit that what morality requires of us is not what we always and necessarily have most reason to do. This is due to the fact that our non-moral considerations may also have strong normative weight that can in some circumstances overrule our moral considerations (see Dorsey 2012: 8; Sobel 20007: 14).

There are stronger and weaker versions of the rejection of morality's overridingness. Susan Wolf, for example, has claimed that in some instances our non-moral concerns outweigh moral considerations to such an extent that adhering to the demands of morality would count as irrational. This means that the non-moral consideration is so normatively weighty that when deciding what we ought to do, the conflicting moral consideration loses its rational force, such that adhering to what morality requires of us would be the *wrong* thing to do (Wolf 1982; Singer 1993: 320-32; Dorsey 2012: 10).

Dale Dorsey adopts a weaker version of this position, accepting that morality will always act as a 'constraint' on our actions when deciding what we ought to do, which means that adhering to a moral requirement will never be 'irrational' or 'wrong' in the way that Wolf suggests. Instead, Dorsey merely claims that in some circumstances we will have good reasons to act contrary to what morality demands of us, due to the fact that our non-moral considerations are significantly normatively weighty (Dorsey 2012: 12-13; Stroud: 176). In this way, the reasons that we have to be moral are always sufficient for action, but in some cases this reason to act morally will not amount to an all-things-considered reason to do what is morally required. As a result, the demandingness of morality is mitigated due to the fact that morality is not considered as rationally authoritative over one's normatively weighty, deeply held non-moral commitments.

However, even if this response to the purported demandingness of morality's overridingness was successful, I argue that a moral obligation could still be determined as over-demanding, and as such, the overridingness objection does not capture the reasons why a moral obligation ought to be considered as over-demanding. This is because even if morality is not rationally authoritative over one's non-moral concerns, we still have to determine which non-moral concerns are normatively weighty enough to trump one's moral obligations. As Dorsey himself claims, in order to determine when a moral consideration can be overridden by one's non-moral concerns, we have to determine when "morality requires significant prudential sacrifice on part of the agents", and this means that "the project of determining when moral requirements fail to be dispositive [rationally authoritative], *just is* the project of determining when moral obligations become too demanding" (Dorsey 2012: 14, emphasis added). In other words, even though Dorsey has provided justification for why it is plausible for moral requirements to sometimes be overridden by non-moral concerns, he does not provide a case for when or why one's non-moral concerns may legitimately trump one's moral requirements. To provide such a case, we need to have an account of when one's non-moral concerns are normatively weighty enough to trump one's moral requirements, and this is determined by examining what counts as an unreasonable sacrifice of one's non-moral commitments.

To assess whether a moral requirement is over-demanding, such as the moral obligation to develop one's talents, we need to determine when doing so would require unreasonable prudential sacrifice. Even though we have responded to the worry of morality's overridingness, this has not helped us to determine whether the obligation to develop one's talents is too demanding, because we are still left with the question of when such an obligation would require an unreasonable sacrifice of our personal commitments. To do this, we need to provide an explanation of what counts as a significant prudential sacrifice, and to assess whether such a sacrifice will arise when an agent fulfils her moral obligation to develop her talents. Rejecting moral rationalism cannot help us to provide such an account.

Therefore, it cannot be that the overridingness objection really captures the reasons why we consider a moral obligation to be over-demanding. This is because it is a conceptual possibility that an obligation could be over-demanding in a way that the overridingness objection does not accommodate for. Even after considering both responses to the overridingness objection, by rejecting morality's overridingness or incorporating one's non-moral commitments into the moral sphere, we can still question whether one's non-moral concerns justifiably override one's moral concerns. Consequently, if the moral obligation to develop one's talents is over-demanding, this demandingness should not be understood in terms of overridingness. Instead, I argue that we need a demandingness objection that helps us to determine when one's deeply held normative commitments are weighty enough to trump the moral concerns in favour of developing one's talent. To provide such an account we have to look to the substantive normative commitments that come with one's talent development, and the way in which these commitments fit with one's non-moral concerns. I will go on to argue for such an account in the next section.

4.4. Demandingness and Endorsement

The content-based demandingness objection that I propose against the moral obligation to develop one's talents is stated as follows: moral obligation T is unreasonably demanding for agent A if and only if compliance with the normative commitments necessary to bring about T requires the unreasonable sacrifice of at least one of A's morally permissible deep normative commitments.[43] This demandingness objection can hold irrespective of the commitments of a particular moral theory, and irrespective of whether morality is deemed to be rationally authoritative over one's non-moral concerns. I have already explained the nature

---

[43] This formulation of the demandingness objection is a version of Braddock's objection from 'cost': "Moral view V is mistaken because it is too demanding in the sense that compliance with its implied obligations would require that we (as compliant agents) sacrifice G, where G consists of a set of goods such as: (i) a significant level of our well-being, (ii) our well-being to the point of view where we fall below the threshold of a minimally decent life, (iii) our central projects, and (iv) highly important objective goods" (Braddock: 170-171). My account of the demandingness objection differs slightly from Braddock's, as I will go on to argue that the moral obligation to develop one's talents is overly demanding insofar as it requires one to sacrifice one's deep normative commitments. These commitments could potentially be classed as 'central projects', consist of important objective goods, and significantly reduce an agent's well-being if not acknowledged, in the way that Braddock proposes.

of one's deep normative commitments: they are one's and personal commitments that bestow meaning and significance to one's life. I now go on to explain when sacrificing these deeply held normative commitments, in favour of fulfilling one's moral obligation to develop one's talents, counts as *unreasonable*. In doing so, I refer to the endorsement constraint I presented in the previous Chapter.

4.4.1. Well-Being and Demandingness

To determine whether adhering to a particular moral requirement counts as unreasonably demanding for an agent, the strategy that most commonly appears in the literature is to determine how such adherence will affect an agent's level of well-being. If an agent's level of well-being falls below a certain threshold, then the sacrifice in well-being is deemed overly demanding. Murphy, for example, offers his account of the 'factual status-quo'; he claims that in order to determine the level of demandingness that is required by a moral requirement, we ought to compare a person's level of well-being before complying with the requirement, with the agent's level of well-being during and after complying with the requirement. In this account, we take "an agent's *actual* situation as given" and then compare "how far his well-being is affected from the time he begins to fully comply with the moral [requirement]" (Murphy: 35, 164-165). When applying this factual status-quo to the potential demandingness of the moral obligation to develop one's talents, we would need to determine how developing one's talents may result in a reduction in one's level of well-being.

In the last Chapter I argued that developing one's talents can conflict with our deep normative commitments. When we develop a talent, there come with it certain required standards and commitments that have to be met in order to successfully bring about that development. These commitments can either be internal or external to the process of developing a particular talent, and they are normative, giving an agent reasons for acting in a particular way. If these commitments do not fit with one's deeply held personal commitments, a conflict will arise that has the potential to significantly reduce one's well-being.

This reduction in well-being can be understood in terms of what Railton has called 'alienation', referring to the reduction in well-being that arises due to a lack of fit between a certain state of affairs (in this case, talent development) and an agent's deep normative commitments (Railton 1984: 134). As previously explained in Chapter Three, the loss that is experienced due to a conflict with one's deeply help personal concerns can be explained by appeal to different values, for example, in terms of autonomy, integrity or authenticity. Whatever value we appeal to, however, being alienated from one's deep normative commitments just means that the agent has to compromise a significant and meaningful part of her life, a part which defines who she is and shapes her conception of the good life. If the development of an agent's talents conflicts with her deeply held normative commitments, then this development will compromise something that is part of the agent that authoritatively provides significance and meaning to her life. This compromise is demanding, resulting in a reduction of an agent's level of well-being.

Just because developing one's talents may conflict with one's deep normative commitments and is as such considered to be personally demanding, this does not mean that the resulting demandingness caused by this alienation is *unreasonable*. As discussed in the previous chapter, it might be that the alienation an agent feels when acting contrary to her deep normative commitments is in fact a good thing, such that the agent *should* be alienated from her deeply held personal commitments. It might be the case, for instance, that an agent's personal commitments encourage her to act in a way that is morally impermissible, or that the agent is mistaken about what she really does value as part of her deeply held convictions (Moseley: 66; Railton 1984: 147). This means that any resulting alienation from these personal commitments would be in the service of avoiding immoral and imprudent behaviour, and would not be considered as over-demanding.

In this way, the 'factual status-quo' that is offered by Murphy, to help determine when a reduction in well-being counts as an *unreasonable* reduction, fails to capture those instances when people's actual level of well-being before complying with a moral obligation is constituted by personal commitments that are deemed as immoral or imprudent. If someone's commitments give rise to immoral or imprudent behaviour, then a reduction in well-being that arises from refraining from this behaviour should not count as unreasonably costly or over-demanding. For example, it may be that fully complying with a particular moral demand will require slave-owner Michael to sell his slaves. If this causes a reduction in Michael's well-being, this reduction should not count as unreasonably costly for Michael: he should not have owned slaves in the first place given that doing so is morally impermissible. Instead, it should be specified that alienation causes unreasonable coasts only if our deeply held commitments are legitimate. This is to adopt a 'normative status-quo', whereby a loss in well-being caused by foregoing immoral and imprudent behaviour does not count as an *unreasonable* loss (Sin: 166; Hooker 2009).

It could be objected that this normatively loaded way of determining what counts as an unreasonable sacrifice potentially begs the question. The normative status-quo is meant to determine when an agent's compromise of her deep normative commitments is unreasonable. However, if we adopt the normative status-quo then what counts as unreasonably demanding will depend on the various commitments of the particular moral theory that we are appealing to. This is because some non-moral commitments will have to be classed as morally impermissible and in order for this to be determined, we need to already know what counts as reasonably demanding. In order to determine whether an agent's non-moral commitments are morally permissible, we already need to have an account of which moral requirements involve an unreasonable sacrifice of our deep normative commitments, because these are the moral requirements that are meant to tell us whether the non-moral concerns counts as morally permissible. But this is exactly what the normative status-quo account is meant to tell us (Sin: 167; Hooker 2009).

To explain further, take the example of Genghis Khan, whose deep normative commitments involve the development of his talent for killing innocent people. Khan's level of well-being is determined by his deep normative commitments that are morally impermissible, and so we do not want to say that a reduction in his well-being caused by him giving up these morally impermissible commitments is unreasonably costly for him. However, in order to arrive at the claim that alienation from Khan's personal commitments *does not* count as an unreasonable sacrifice, we have to be able to claim that Khan's non-moral commitments are not normatively weighty enough to trump the moral demand to refrain from killing innocent people. The normative status-quo was meant to provide a way to make such an assessment, that the non-moral concerns are not normatively weighty or whether or not the relevant moral concerns are not normatively weighty. But by providing a normative threshold which excludes certain non-moral concerns due to their being morally unacceptable, there may be a worry that we are already assuming what we are meant to be arguing for. It seems like we might have in place an idea about which moral concerns are too demanding or which non-moral concerns are weight enough to trump certain moral concerns, and this is just to assume what the normative status-quo was meant to determine.

We can respond to this worry, however, by highlighting that we expect Khan to refrain from developing his talent for killing innocent people because doing so was not considered to be morally permissible. This means that the obligation to develop his talent conflicted with other moral requirements of the moral theory. As a result, there would in fact be no *prima facie* moral obligation for Khan to develop his talents in the first place, and the reason why Khan's alienation counts as a reasonable sacrifice is because there is in fact no requirement for him to develop his talents; morality places no such demand on him. The point is that the development of Khan's talent is not morally *permissible*, let alone morally *required*.

If a moral theory *does* require a person to develop their talents, given the fact that doing so does not conflict with the other moral commitments of that theory, then we have to assume that the moral theory is internally consistent in prescribing such an obligation, otherwise, there would be no such moral requirement to do so. In this way, we would always have a *moral* reason to develop our talents if doing so was morally required of us, and there is nothing suspicious about prescribing that one's deeply held normative commitments ought to be morally permissible if their sacrifice counts as unreasonably costly; it is up to the particular moral theory in question to provide an account of what is morally permissible in each case. Our concern with demandingness does not touch on what a morally theory *allows*, but only what a moral theory *demands*, and presumably, if a moral theory *demands* something, then it necessarily also has to be *allowed* in the first place.

Given that an agent's deeply held normative commitments are morally permissible, and given that they conflict with her moral obligation to develop her talents, the question now stands how we determine whether that conflict counts as an unreasonable sacrifice in well-being. I propose that this can be determined by referring to the endorsement constraint, stated as follows:

> *Demandingness Endorsement Constraint.* The moral obligation to develop one's talent *T* is reasonably demanding for agent *A* if and only if *A* endorses (or would endorse if under optimal decision-making conditions) the normative requirements necessary to bring about *T*, as part of or complimentary to *A*'s (morally permissibly) deeply held normative commitments.

If the endorsement constraint is not met, then the moral obligation to develop one's talents is overly demanding. For the remainder of this chapter, I will argue for my claim that the endorsement constraint is necessary for determining whether the moral requirement to develop one's talents constitutes an unreasonable sacrifice of well-being.

4.4.2. The Endorsement Constraint Revisited

So far I have argued that if the normative commitments required to bring about the development of one's talent conflict with one's deeply held personal commitments, then this will result in alienation, and a reduction of one's well-being. This alienation occurs because one's personal commitments are significant enough to bestow one's life with meaning and shape one's sense of who one is and the values one holds. Having to act contrary to these commitments would be highly costly in terms of well-being. The question remains, however, as to whether this cost in well-being counts as unreasonably demanding.

In the last chapter I argued for the endorsement constraint, claiming that for talent development to be a constitutive part of one's well-being, the agent must endorse the commitments that are necessarily required to bring about the development of her talent as complimentary to or part of her deeply held personal commitments. The agent's endorsement is a necessary part of what makes talent development prudentially good, and without the agent's endorsement, doing so would not be prudentially good for her.

I also argue that the endorsement constraint is necessary when determining whether the moral obligation to develop one's talents is overly demanding. This is because the demandingness objection that I have been advocating thus far understands demandingness in terms of an agent's level of well-being. Given the endorsement constraint, developing one's talent does not contribute to one's well-being unless one also endorses the requirements that are necessary to bring about the development of one's talent. As such, developing a talent, the commitments of which you do not endorse, is not good for you and will result in a lack of fit with one's own deeply held personal commitments. That is to say, this lack of endorsement will result in a significant reduction in one's well-being. This reduction in well-being is a result of the alienation that is caused when an agent acts contrary to the commitments in her life that give her meaning and define her sense of who she is. Disregarding these personal commitments will always be unreasonably costly in terms of well-being. As such, the agent's endorsement of the normative commitments that come with the development of her talent is necessary for that development to count as reasonably demanding.

It could be objected, however, that endorsement cannot play such a significant role in determining whether the moral obligation to develop one's talents is unreasonably demanding. Take this case as an example. Tom has a talent for scientific research, and given an outbreak of a deadly disease X, Tom is asked by the World Health Organisation to leave his family behind and give up his career as a gardener to help find the cure for X. Furthermore, according to the moral theory that Tom, and for the sake of this example, we all adhere to, Tom is morally required to do what the World Health Organisation asks of him. Tom decides, however, that developing his scientific talent does not fit with his own deep normative commitments. As a result, after considered reflection under the optimal conditions that are conducive to making good decisions about his well-being and conception of the good, Tom does not endorse the normative commitments that come with the further development of his talent. Under my account of the demandingness objection, this means that the moral obligation for Tom to develop his talent is unreasonably demanding.

However, morality sometimes requires us to do things that aren't always prudentially beneficial. For example, I may be morally required to give my friend the money that I owe her and I may be required to donate a percentage of my salary or volunteer some of my time to helping those who are in need, even though this means I have to neglect some other prudential commitments. The fact that what morality requires may be contrary to what I endorse, does not necessarily give me an authoritative reason to act contrary to what morality requires. This means that Tom's lack of endorsement of his talent development does not mean that the moral obligation to do so is unreasonably demanding; the demandingness may in fact be reasonable. The objection, therefore, claims that a lack of endorsement cannot tell us that demandingness is unreasonable, as opposed to the reasonable kind that is accepted of morality more generally.

To respond to this objection, it is important to stress that one's endorsement does not appeal to mere 'wants' or 'likes' or 'desires'. The endorsement constraint does not justify Tom deciding to act against his moral obligation to develop his talent merely on a whim, or because he preferred spending time with his family or continuing his career as a gardener rather than acting to prevent the spread of disease *X*. Endorsement is a considered reflection about the fit of the normative commitments that are necessary for the development of one's talent, with one's own deeply held personal commitments. These personal commitments are normative and give value and meaning to one's life, provide reasons for action and shape one's conception of the good life. Acting contrary to these deeply held commitments is just to take away one's meaning, one's reasons for actions, and to impose central projects that go against one's conception of the good life. This kind of personal imposition does not necessarily arise when morality merely asks of an agent to give up material goods, for example, by giving more money to charity or paying more taxes in order to fund a social welfare system. One does not necessarily have to compromise one's character or sense of who one is in order to make material sacrifices.

If an action or state of affairs conflicts with one's deep normative commitments, then something has gone *prima facie* wrong – an agent's sense of self and meaning in her life should not be compromised lightly. Such a violation has serious normative consequences. For example, a caring and loving parent would find it extremely painful to act in such a way that hindered and neglected the well-being of her children; this is because as a parent, one's deeply held normative commitments include the conviction to care for the welfare of one's child. If developing one's talent meant that this would harm one's child in some way, or hinder the parental relationship with one's child, then this would count as a conflict with one's deeply held normative commitments. This conflict would have to be taken very seriously when deciding what one has an all-things-considered reason to do.

As such, the reduction in Tom's well-being if he developed his talent would be significantly costly to his well-being – it would be an imposition on his character and his ability to determine and live by his own conception of what is meaningful in his life. This cost and imposition is therefore only reasonable if he endorses the normative commitments that are necessary for the development of his talent as fitting with his deeply held personal commitments.

It could still be argued that there may be cases in which even this costly sacrifice to one's well-being does not override the moral requirement to develop one's talents. It may the case, therefore, that Tom *should* compromise his deeply held personal commitments by neglecting his career and his family, and instead develop his scientific talents so as to prevent the spread of the deadly disease. For example, in emergency situations such as war-time or severe health epidemics, what is morally required of us is expected to be extreme and highly-demanding. Under these circumstances there may times in which we would expect that a person ought to change who they are and neglect their deeply held commitments; for example, during the Second World War, British citizens were expected to forgo family and career commitments in order to help with the war effort.

I do not necessarily deny this; in these emergency situations morality may be extremely demanding, and this demandingness may be reasonable irrespective of agent's lack of endorsement of the commitments that come with the moral requirements. For the purposes of the arguments that I have presented thus far, I have been assuming that the normal moral situation we find ourselves in every day is not an emergency in this way. Some consequentialists have argued contrary to this assumption, claiming that the world in which we currently live *does* require extreme morality, such that we ought to consider ourselves as living in emergency-like situations given the severe inequality of resources and welfare that is apparent in different parts of the world (Singer 1972). However, not all consequentialists argue in this strong way (see for example Railton 1984), and furthermore, there have been recent real-life cases that mitigate such a strong claim. For example, the recent Ebola outbreak in West Africa was considered to be an emergency situation by the World Health Organisation, and nurses and doctors from all countries were encouraged to donate their time to volunteer in support of the relief efforts. However, it is one thing to say that these nurses and doctors were doing something morally praiseworthy, and quite another to say that they were morally obligated to neglect their meaningful personal commitments to risk their lives to stop the spread of Ebola. As such, even in emergency situations, we can still consider these acts to be supererogatory, rather than morally demanded of us.[44]

Therefore, the endorsement constraint is applicable in all but the most severe emergency situations in which normal moral and societal conventions are disrupted. Under these conditions, the moral obligation to develop one's talents will only be classed as reasonably demanding insofar as an agent endorses the normative commitments that are necessarily required in order to bring about her compliance with that obligation. With that said, it is important to highlight that the endorsement constraint is a condition specifically on the reasonableness of the moral demand to develop one's talents, and does not specify a constraint on *all* moral requirements. My view, therefore, leaves room for the fact that there may be some moral obligations that are not constrained by an agent's endorsement of the normative commitments necessarily required to comply with that obligation. The endorsement constraint does however constrain what morality can demand of an agent with regards to the development of her talents. As a result, the demandingness objection with regards to the moral obligation to develop one's talents is plausibly grounded in the endorsement constraint. In the

---

[44] I will leave for further research the question of the role that the endorsement constraint plays in determining what is required of us all-things-considered in emergency situations like the ones that I have just described. In the meantime, for an interesting discussion of emergency morality see Sorrell (2003).

next section I respond to three further objections that can be raised against my formulation of demandingness objection, understood in terms of the endorsement constraint.

4.5. Three Further Objections

Objection One. It has been argued that the demandingness objection mistakenly assumes a clear distinction between moral reasons and non-moral reasons. Such a distinction is argued to be implausible given the fact the moral and non-moral spheres do not involve distinct points of view or appeal to a distinct and unique set of reasons (Crisp 1997; Raz 1986, 2000; Bagnoli: 3). However, my formulation of the demandingness objection does not rely on carving up moral and non-moral considerations into distinct domains. As I have argued, the demandingness objection with regards to the moral obligation to develop one's talents is still conceivable *even if* we incorporate our non-moral concerns into the moral sphere, or even if we consider our non-moral and moral commitments as distinct. If the moral obligation to develop one's talents is over-demanding, it is because it involves an unreasonable reduction in an agent's well-being. Whether this reduction is considered part of the moral sphere or the non-moral sphere, a combination of both, or even if such a distinction cannot be made, this does not affect the plausibility of the arguments offered in this chapter. The demandingness objection still holds irrespective of how we name or categorise the sphere in which one's deeply held personal commitments belong.

Objection Two. The demandingness objection has been objected to based on the fact that it is thought to merely rely on intuitions about what counts as reasonable for an agent to sacrifice. The problem with this is that our intuitions are often unreliable and grounded on a socialisation process that is indexed to the way in which we have been brought up and influenced by those around us (Braddock: 175). This means that the demandingness objection is based on highly contingent intuitions that are unstable, unreliable, and often distorted (Berkey: 3018-3023). However, the demandingness objection that I raise with regards to the moral obligation to develop one's talents is not grounded on an appeal to intuition, but on the endorsement constraint which, as I have argued, relies on an agent's considered judgement regarding the fit of her personal commitments with the development of her talent.

Objection Three. David Sobel has further argued against the demandingness objection on the grounds that by itself, the objection does not do any substantial work in rejecting a particular moral theory. Focussing on consequentialism, Sobel argues that the demandingness objection already assumes various anti-consequentialist intuitions in order to get off the ground, and so cannot by itself be a rejection of consequentialism. This means that if we are at all persuaded by the demandingness objection, it is because we have already rejected the substantive claims of consequentialism, the theory that we were trying to argue was over-demanding. Sobel claims that to formulate the demandingness objection we would, for example, already have had to normatively distinguish between the costs to the person who is required to perform the action, and the cost to the person who is meant to benefit from the action. But consequentialism does not make this substantive distinction and is committed to the claim that in fact such a distinction cannot be made (Sobel 2007: 4).

Sobel's objection is not a problem for the demandingness objection that I present with regards to the moral obligation to develop one's talents. This is for two reasons. First, it is not clear that all consequentialists do not distinguish between the cost to the giver and the cost to the receiver, such that there is no significant weight given to the personal cost involved for the agent who is required to act. This is evident in those variations of consequentialism that incorporate one's non-moral concerns in the moral sphere (Railton 1984; Scheffler 1994). Sobel's objection is thus only relevant to a very small group of moral theories. Furthermore, my iteration of the demandingness objection does not focus on one particular moral theory, but the content of the moral obligation to develop one's talents. This means my demandingness objection holds no matter which moral theory is being scrutinised.

Second, the demandingness objection that I propose does not merely assume that an agent's sacrifice when carrying out the moral obligation to develop her talents is unreasonably costly – it argues for this and explains why the demandingness objection should hold. I have argued why we should consider as problematic the reduction in well-being that occurs when developing one's talents conflicts with one's deep normative commitments, and why this reduction is enough to render the moral obligation to develop one's talents as unreasonably demanding. As such, Sobel's objection does not hold against the demandingness objection that I have argued for in this chapter.

4.6. Conclusion

In this chapter I have argued that if a moral theory is to plausibly claim that an agent has a moral obligation to develop her talents, then that obligation will be conditional on the agent's endorsement of the normative commitments that are required to bring about the development of her talents. Without this endorsement, the development of one's talent is unreasonably demanding.

There are two different ways in which to understand how this endorsement constraint places a condition on whether or not one has a moral obligation to develop one's talents. This difference depends on whether or not we accept morality as overriding. On the one hand, we might be moral rationalists and accept that morality overrides one's non-moral concerns when deciding what we ought to do all-things-considered. In trying to avoid the over-demandingness objection, we would attempt to incorporate deeply held non-moral concerns into the moral sphere. If this is the case, and the agent does not endorse the development of her talent, then the moral obligation to do so will only be *prima facie*, as no such obligation would be generated from the moral theory in the first place.

On the other hand, we might deny the fact that morality is authoritative over our non-moral concerns and, for example, follow Dorsey's view that non-moral concerns can trump moral ones on the occasions when they are sufficiently normatively weighty. If this is the case, and a moral theory requires that an agent ought to develop her talents, then this obligation will be *pro tanto*; the agent's endorsement is relevant here when determining whether she ought to comply with this obligation all-things-considered. As such, if an agent does not endorse the commitments necessary to bring about the development of her talent, the *pro tanto* moral obligation can be overridden insofar as it is overly demanding. Therefore, the demandingness objection that I propose will place conditions on either the *pro tanto* obligation or the *all-things-considered* obligation to develop one's talents, depending on whether or not we accept morality's purported overridingness over one's non-moral concerns.

At this point there are a few general conclusions that can be drawn from the last three chapters, regarding the potential obligation and reasons that one may have to develop one's talents. First, both Kant and moral perfectionists explicitly claim that there is a moral duty to develop one's talents; this is because doing so was considered to be necessary for the development of one's moral agency. However, in Chapters Two and Three I argued that these two theories cannot in fact generate from their commitments the moral obligation to develop one's talents – it is not true that talent development is necessary for the preservation and perfection of one's moral agency. In Chapter Three I further argued that welfare perfectionists cannot plausibly claim that developing one's talent is objectively prudentially good and constitutive of an agent's flourishing. This is because the claim that we have good prudential reasons to develop our talents is conditional on meeting the endorsement constraint. Welfare perfectionism as it stands does not meet this condition. (But a plausible version of hybrid perfectionism might).

In this chapter I argued that endorsement also acts as a constraint on the reasonable demandingness of the potential moral obligation to develop one's talents. Without an agent's endorsement, the moral obligation to develop her talents is unreasonably demanding. This means that whether or not an agent has a moral obligation to develop her talent is conditional on the agent's endorsement of that development. If we are moral rationalists then the endorsement constraint places a condition on whether or not the obligation is *pro tanto,* and if we reject moral rationalism then the endorsement constraint places a condition on whether the obligation is one we ought to comply with *all-things-considered.* In the next chapter I move on to focus on the relationship between talent development and the value of equality, and how we ought to respond to the problem of unequal talents.

Chapter Five

Talents and Equality

5.1. Introduction

So far I have argued that for talent development to be a constitutive part of one's well-being, or morally required, then one has to endorse the normative commitments that are necessary to bring about the development of one's talent, as specified by the endorsement constraint. If there is no such endorsement, the development of one's talent is not prudentially good, and the moral obligation to develop one's talents is unreasonably demanding.

In this chapter I turn to the social and political questions that arise when considering the role that talents play in our lives. The resources produced and consumed by identifying and utilising our talents will often impact on how resources are distributed and social institutions are organised. Given that a talent allows a person to more efficiently and uniquely develop a particular set of skills, this social impact is often thought to be positive, in a way that talent development is considered to be beneficial for society, allowing social institutions to function more productively and efficiently.

There is widespread consensus, therefore, that the state has good reason to identify talents in its citizens and to encourage their development, either directly or indirectly. This is illustrated by the increasingly commonplace talent development programmes within commercial and social institutions; for example, the government-funded 'UK Sport' now boasts their "biggest ever" talent identification and development programme (UK Sport 2015), the national arts bodies of both England and Scotland have stated that talent development programmes are of primary importance,[45] and in the commercial sector, the

---

[45] See Arts Council England's latest '10-Year Strategic Framework', in which it is claimed that "[t]alent is our primary resource", and that they aim to "[i]nvest in arts organisations that are committed to the development of artistic talent" (Arts Council England 2017).

debate surrounding how best to attract and manage talent has become increasingly fashionable, with consulting firms such as McKinsey & Company and PwC offering services that claim to aid clients in their attempt to 'win the war for talent'.[46] As such, institutionalised talent programmes are a commonplace feature of most contemporary western societies, thought to garner widespread positive benefits.

Institutionalised talent identification and development may give rise to positive benefits. However, egalitarians worry that it may also unjustly disrupt levels of social equality, because recognising some levels of ability specifically as 'talents', and encouraging their further development, is just to identify unfair inequalities in ability and to further propagate the arising unequal advantages. When the state becomes involved, the acknowledgement and proliferation of unequal talents is institutionally accepted, endorsed and acted upon. Even though we may endorse the commitments that come with the development of our talents, and even if doing so is morally required or a constitutive part of our well-being, egalitarianism thus tells us that we ought to be sensitive to the fact that talents are unequally distributed in society – it is just a brute fact that some people are more talented than others. This egalitarian concern gives rise to an axiological tension; on the one hand, we recognise the value in identifying and developing our talents, but on the other hand, doing so potentially gives rise to inequalities that are unjust.

Given the fact of unequal talents and the egalitarian challenge that this poses, in this chapter I examine how we ought to answer to this egalitarian challenge and how best to counteract the problem of unequal talents. To do so I focus on the debate between two prominent, yet contrasting accounts of egalitarianism, luck egalitarianism on the one hand, and relational egalitarianism on the other, adjudicating which theory best argues for how we ought to

---

See also Creative Scotland's 10-year plan, 'Unlocking Potential, Embracing Ambition', which sets out as a priority the "support [of] emerging talent" and to encourage organisations to "develop talent and skills" (Creative Scotland 2014).

[46] See for example McKinsey & Company's 'Human Capital' department, which aims to help clients "turn talent into a source of competitive advantage" (McKinsey & Company 2017), and PwC's talent management program which claims to provide clients with the means to "attract and retain talented people" (PwC 2017).

counteract the disadvantages caused by unequal levels of talent. The theory that offers the best response, I claim, will be the theory that most plausibly frames *why* unequal talents disrupt levels of equality, and why any arising inequalities count as unjust.

Luck egalitarians claim that inequalities in talent are unjust when they are a matter of bad brute luck and disrupt a person's comparative level of advantage, whilst relational egalitarians claim that these inequalities are unjust when they disrupt the equality of 'relational' goods. I argue that even though some unequal advantages arising from unequal talents may be 'relational', this does not mean that we ought to adopt the theory of relational egalitarianism in order to explain why inequalities in talent are unjust, or how we ought to counteract these inequalities. This is because relational egalitarianism is misguided when it comes to assessing why we value talents and the advantages that developing our talents can give us. In light of this, I propose that luck egalitarianism provides a more plausible account of how to respond to the problem of unequal talents, a response which is informed by the luck egalitarian account of why unequal talents are unjust.

The structure of the chapter will be as follows. In the next section I analyse why talents matter for egalitarian justice, and what grounds the egalitarian challenge posed by unequal talents. In doing so I refer back to the account of the nature and value of talent that I developed in Chapter One. In Section Three I outline the luck egalitarian position regarding the distribution of unequal talents, and in Section Four I discuss the relational egalitarian position, illustrating two ways in which relational inequalities may arise from unequal levels of talent. In Section Five I argue that luck egalitarians can in fact successfully accommodate these relational inequalities into their own view, and in some respects do so more effectively than relational egalitarians themselves. As a result, in Section Six I make a case for my claim that luck egalitarianism, rather than relational egalitarianism, offers a more plausible account of how to counteract the injustices that arise from unequal talents. Luck egalitarians advocate a neutralisation approach, which I argue most plausibly captures the reasons for why unequal talents disrupt levels of equality, and why the arising inequalities count as unjust. In Section Seven I conclude.

5.2. Why Unequal Talents Matter

Given that some people are more talented than others, levels of talent are distributed unequally in society. In the literature on egalitarian justice, discussion of unequal talents has centred on the question of the nature of this inequality, and the extent to which these inequalities are considered to be unjust. However, despite the fact that this debate has been ongoing for some time now, it is often not clear what is meant by the notion of a talent, why talents are considered to be valuable, and as such, why talents matter for concerns of egalitarian justice. Before going on to present my case for luck egalitarianism, it is therefore important to resolve this ambiguity and clearly state why unequal talents are thought to disrupt equality.

There are two ways in which this ambiguity about the nature and value of talent presents itself in the existing literature. First, there is a conceptual incoherence; as I highlighted in Chapter One, the word 'talent' is often used as synonymous with the words 'ability', 'endowment' and 'capacity'. Dworkin and Rawls, for example, use the words 'talent', 'ability' and 'skill' interchangeably (Dworkin 2000: 92, 97; Rawls 1999: 63, 73), Cohen refers synonymously to a talent as a 'capacity', and Anderson considers a talent to be an 'endowment' (Cohen 2011: 30; Anderson 1999: 302). Although these differences could be interpreted as a mere terminological oversight, there is in fact a substantive issue at stake. Abilities and skills, on the one hand, are usually considered to be personal competencies that have already been nurtured or developed to some extent. Capacities and endowments, on the other hand, are considered to be dispositional potential for a skill or ability that has yet to be expressed or cultivated. Both ways of referring to a talent highlight an attractive or significant aspect of what a talent might be. However, whichever definition we adopt will have different implications for how we understand the nature of the inequalities that arise from unequal talents.

In Chapter One I argued for an account of talent understood as a dispositional quality, a high level of potential for a particular skill that is manifested and expressed in the excellent acquisition of that skill. A talent is potential that is expressed as an excellence in skill acquisition, and as such, it gives rise to or opens up an opportunity that when nurtured and utilised can give a person access to various kinds of valuable advantages. The fact that talents give rise to valuable opportunities appears to come across as the primary understanding of a 'talent' in the literature on egalitarian justice, although this is far from explicit or obvious. For example, Anderson states that talents are valuable insofar as they are developed into a valuable acquisition of certain skills, and similarly Dworkin claims that talents offer the potential for future success once they have been nurtured (Anderson 2007: 615; Dworkin 2000: 92). As such, talents are valued due to the fact that they can be advantageously developed. This does not rule out that the talent may already have been developed to some extent, but only specifies that the value of a talent is indexed to the fact that they can be developed and nurtured, and that this development is advantageous.

It is important to emphasise that talents are not only valued as the potential to develop *any* skill. Instead, as Dworkin claims, we value talents for the opportunities that they give us to develop a skill that proves to be advantageous for the individual who possesses it, allowing them to flourish and succeed (Dworkin 2000: 92). Rawls too considers a talent to be an 'asset', suggesting that talents have the potential to offer some kind of useful benefit if developed, both for the talented individual and for those around her; in this way, Rawls claims that talents have 'exchange value' (Rawls 1999: 63). This value can be explained by the account of talents I presented in Chapter One: talents allow a person to more efficiently, productively and uniquely develop a particular set of skills, and the way in which a person benefits from their talent will in part depend on contingent facts about the type of skill that is developed, the way in which one's society values that skill, and how the comparison thresholds are set for calculating what counts as a 'superior' ability. As a result, the value of a talent is sensitive to the axiological commitments of one's society.

Talents therefore give a person access to various kinds of personal and social advantages when they are developed, and this value often rests on already existing social arrangements and commitments. It is because talents are valued in this way that they are significant for accounts of egalitarian justice; we worry about unequal levels of talent in society as being *prima facie* unjust because it signals a social inequality in something that matters to us, something that may give us valuable and advantageous opportunities that are important for the way in which we successfully live our lives.

The second ambiguity that arises in the literature regarding the nature and value of talents is based on an assumption about how talents emerge in the first place. It is widely assumed by most egalitarians that talents are something 'genetic', 'natural', or 'inborn', and that these 'native' qualities are merely expressed by the relevant social environments in which a person finds herself (see Kymlicka 1990: 61-80; Dworkin 2000: 65-119; Cohen 2011: 19, 30; Anderson 1999: 302). Given this, the question that is often asked in the literature is how society ought to deal with arising inequalities in 'natural' talents once they have already emerged. Seeing as talents are 'natural', there is nothing that society can do but mitigate any negative social effects that materialise from unequal levels of talent.

However, as I argued in Chapter One, the scientific evidence makes it clear that this 'naturalist' way of understanding the emergence of talents is incorrect. It is not the case that talents are natural, but instead one's genetic make-up and social environment dynamically interact to play a constitutive role in the way that talents are formed (Fishkin: 115). One's genes are not merely expressed, but are also constructed in response to one's surrounding social environment. This means that social structures can directly shape one's genetic predisposition, and therefore, one's level of talent. Therefore, talents are not merely 'natural' or 'inborn' but are in part a direct product of one's social environment.

This means that one's social opportunities can affect a person's level of talent before and after they are born, and by the time we come to initially identify and assess levels of talent there will have already been normatively significant social interactions that have shaped one's level of potential for a particular skill. The focus in the egalitarian debate with regards to how 'natural' talents are to be mitigated is therefore misguided. It is not the fact that a person is born with a level of talent and only after this fact is society asked to deal with the arising inequalities. Instead, the mere fact that there are unequal levels of talent also points to the fact that people have experienced unequal levels of formative and developmental experiences in their social environment; a person's level of talent is as much a symptom of both natural *and* social factors. The egalitarian debate should not only ask how society ought to be organised given unequal levels of talent, but how society ought to be organised so as to respond to unequal levels of talent in the first place.

By making clear the way in which we should understand the notion of a talent and why talents are valuable, this has made explicit why unequal levels of talent should matter for egalitarian justice – talents give rise to inequalities in advantageous opportunities for development. Arriving at this claim has been important, not just to provide clarity for what follows, but also because the arguments I present later in the chapter to support luck egalitarianism rest on an account of why talents are valuable and how unequal levels of talent disrupt levels of social equality. In the next section I begin by explaining the basic commitments of luck egalitarianism, and why it considers levels of talent to be something that ought to be distributed equally in society.

5.3. Luck Egalitarianism and Unequal Talents

The version of luck egalitarianism that I adopt and argue for in this chapter can be stated as follows: it is unjust for one to be comparatively disadvantaged with respect to what is valuable in one's life, to the extent that this level of disadvantage is a matter of bad brute luck, both natural and social (Segall: 6). Underlying this claim is the intuition that people should not be disadvantaged through no fault of their own. Because of this, luck egalitarians consider instances of brute luck – luck that arises due to a person's circumstances over which she has no control – to be morally arbitrary, because a person could not have reasonably avoided the effects of this luck and so are not at fault for the arising disadvantages. As Cohen states, the purpose of egalitarian justice is "to eliminate involuntary disadvantage, by which I (stipulatively) mean disadvantage for which the sufferer cannot be held responsible, since it does not appropriately reflect the choices that he has made or is making or would make" (Cohen 2011: 13). In light of this, luck egalitarianism considers the fair and equal organisation of society and allocation of resources to be sensitive to brute luck.[47]

At this point, it is important to make four qualifications to the luck egalitarian position I have just outlined. First, luck egalitarians judge states of affairs and levels of disadvantage *comparatively*; luck and choice only matter if they disrupt levels of distributive equality across members of society. Second, the luck egalitarian concern about inequalities is not triggered by any instance of inequality *tout court*, but only by comparative *disadvantages*. It is only when someone is comparatively disadvantaged by their level of talent, for example, that the luck egalitarian begins to assess whether this disadvantage counts as unjust.[48]

Third, the most attractive luck egalitarian position is one that only kicks in after a basic humanitarian threshold, so that those who are comparatively disadvantaged in such a way that hinders their opportunity to lead a minimally decent life, are given the necessary assistance, irrespective of whether these disadvantages arise as a matter of brute luck (Tan: 100). By including into the theory a minimal threshold only after which the sensitivity to brute luck is relevant, this allows the luck egalitarian to respond to the worry that their theory

---

[47] Some versions of luck egalitarianism focus on whether or not a person is *responsible* for the arising comparative disadvantages (see for example Dworkin 2000). However, for the purposes of this chapter, I need only focus on the fact that luck egalitarians are sensitive to bad brute luck – this allows me to leave aside the question of what counts as responsibility, and whether there is a robust distinction between luck on the one hand, and responsibility on the other.

[48] Luck egalitarians are often criticised for worrying about luck *tout court* on the effect of distributive justice, even when that effect is a relative advantage rather than merely a disadvantage (Schwartz: 253). However, the most plausible and attractive account of luck egalitarianism will only consider as normatively salient the *disadvantages* caused by differential luck, that is, when the luck in question is *bad* luck. To present an argument for this claim is beyond the scope of this chapter; for an already existing discussion in the literature see Shlomi Segall (2013): 40-42; Hirose & Segall (2016): 18; Lippert-Rasmussen (2005): 262.

is unattractively harsh, allowing those who are left destitute due to factors that are not a matter of brute luck, to suffer without assistance (Anderson 1999: 295).[49]

Finally, it also important to qualify that the most attractive version of luck egalitarianism will not make any substantive presuppositions or presumptions about what counts as brute luck. In this sense, the theory is 'thin' rather than 'thick', merely claiming that what counts as an unjust inequality is one that gives rise to a comparative disadvantage that is caused by brute luck. For example, according to Cohen, the luck egalitarian position merely states that "all innate and otherwise (in the broadest sense) inherited differences of advantage are, accordingly unjust" (Cohen 2011: 117), and that "if there is no such thing [as genuine choice] – because, for example "hard determinism" is true – then all differential advantage is unjust" (Cohen 2011: 60). This leaves open the substantial question about what actually counts as matter of brute luck.[50]

When it comes to assessing whether unequal levels of talent count as unjust, the luck egalitarian will therefore appeal to the principle that a person's

---

[49] It will, of course, need to be determined what counts as a minimally decent life and what counts as the minimal threshold below which the luck egalitarian position is not relevant.

[50] It has been objected that appealing to a 'thin' notion of luck might leave the luck egalitarian having to admit that *everything* is a result of brute luck, because the way in which we make choices may in fact be a result of factors that are a matter of brute luck and so beyond our control. If this is the case, then this would contradict the common-sense belief that we can hold people morally responsible for their actions when they have chosen to do something morally wrong (for a version of this objection see for example Scheffler 2005; Colburn 2010; Rawls 1999: 178, 197; Rawls 1993: 13, 19-20; Sher: 410; Dworkin 2000: 7, 323; Mason 2006: 92). However, if it really is true that all choices are made in a way that depends entirely on bad brute luck, then it is strange to think that given this metaphysical truth, we would consider someone in control, and thus responsible, for their choices. Advocates of luck egalitarianism have also responded to this worry by noting that even if it is metaphysically true that the way in which we make choices in entirely a result of bad brute luck, our notion of moral responsibility need not be grounded in this metaphysical claim. Rather, our notion of moral responsibility can be socially determined and prescribed in whatever way is amenable to account for moral blame and praise. This normative account of moral responsibility does not, however, affect the luck egalitarian claim that metaphysically speaking, there may be instances of choice-making that are entirely determined by one's bad brute luck; see for example Kok-Char Tan (2012: 93, 137) and McTernan (2016). Carl Knight (2009; 2013) argues against this kind of move made by advocates of luck egalitarianism.

relative level of advantage should not depend on what is a matter of brute luck. However, there are good reasons to think that a person's level of talent is in fact a result of brute luck *and* factors over which one has control. As I argued in Chapter One, one's talents emerge partly as a result of one's environment, and this environment is also shaped by the way in which one chooses to interact with it. As such, most egalitarians accept that one's level of talent is partly shaped by one's choices and is not merely a result of brute luck.[51] Considering that luck egalitarianism should be understood as a 'thin' theory in the way that I described above, it is not up to the luck egalitarian to determine exactly which part of one's talent is and is not a matter of brute luck. Rather, the luck egalitarian claim is only that given the fact that there is some part of a person's level of talent that is a result of brute luck, any arising comparative disadvantages that are a matter of this brute luck will count as unjust.[52]

Having outlined the luck egalitarian position with regards to unequal talents, in the next section I explain the way in which relational egalitarians account for the injustice of unequal talents. As I will go on to show, even though unequal talents may give rise to an injustice that is relational in nature, this does not mean that relational egalitarianism is the best theory to plausibly frame *why*

---

[51] On this point regarding the intertwining nature between brute luck and choice when it comes to talents, see Anderson: 300; Arneson 1989; Sher: 402; Hurley 2002; Rawls 1999: 312; Cohen 2011: 222; Dworkin 2000: 91. It is also important to note that I am treating Dworkin as a luck-egalitarian for the purposes of this chapter, even though he denies such a label (Dworkin 2003). However, I consider this label as pertinent for sake of argument here, because Dworkin is also sensitive to brute luck when it comes to egalitarian justice and talents, and it is just this sensitivity that I mean to analyse with regards to talent and equality.

[52] It could be argued that because talents emerge as a dynamic and close interaction between one's circumstances (which counts as brute luck) and one's choices, it is epistemologically impossible to actually locate which part of one's talents is and is not a result of brute luck. This would make it impossible for luck egalitarianism to provide a successful account of how to counteract unjust inequalities in talent. However, luck egalitarians just deny that it is epistemologically impossible to do so. Dworkin, for example, offers his hypothetical insurance model and Roemer offers his own 'pragmatic' solution (Dworkin 2000; Roemer 1993). Although these attempts at locating instances of brute luck in the emergence of one's talents can be objected to in their own right (see Cohen 2011: 29 and Fishkin: 61), this does not mean that no such attempt will be successful. The burden of proof is thus on those who make the strong claim that it is *impossible* to successfully locate instances of brute luck.

unequal talents matter to levels of equality, and how we subsequently ought to counteract these inequalities.

5.4. Relational Egalitarianism and Unequal Talents

Relational egalitarians reject the main commitments of luck egalitarianism, claiming that justice should not be thought of in terms of disadvantages caused by bad brute luck. Instead, egalitarian justice ought to measure the way in which citizens and social institutions treat each other (Anderson 2010: 23). Equality is thus understood as a measure of social norms and behaviour, as a "social relation between persons – an equality of authority, status or standing" (Anderson 2010: 1). Relational egalitarians consider the demands of egalitarian justice to be met when people are able to stand in equal relations to each other and participate as equals in political and social institutions. Relational equality is disrupted, therefore, when hierarchical power relations emerge, such as domination, marginalisation and oppression, hindering the equal treatment of citizens (Schemmel: 366). Insofar as the distribution of individual holdings and advantages is important for equality, it is only to serve as a means to construct a society that allows people to engage in relationships that embody equal respect and treatment.

When it comes to talents and their development, the relational egalitarian will therefore claim that the mere fact of an unequal distribution of talent is not *in itself* unjust, but only insofar as it means that people in society are unable to relate to each other as equals, unable to engage in relationships that express equal concern and respect. Unlike the luck egalitarian, who worries about unequal talents to the extent that they hinder someone's relative access to advantage, the relational egalitarian only worries about unequal talents insofar as they disrupt the equality of relational goods – goods that are created or constituted by the way people treat and behave towards each other.

Relational egalitarians reject the luck egalitarian account of talent and equality, because it apparently ignores and does not give grounds for eliminating these relational goods. By focussing on how a person's level of talent affects their individual comparative level of advantage, luck egalitarianism is thought to account merely for goods that can be distributed. Relational goods, however are not these kinds of goods; the reason why someone feels humiliated or inferior is not due to "something that is measurable in individual holdings (something that can be *had*)", but is rather "internal to a relation" and cannot be attached to one person's comparative level of material wealth or advantage (Axelsen & Bidadanure: 9). Relational inequalities are assessed by considering how people are treated and not what people receive as part of their fair shares of goods (Anderson 2010: 6-12). And so, even if there is society in which a distribution of goods has been set up in keeping with the commitments of luck egalitarianism, the relational egalitarian will claim that there are still instances of unjust relational inequalities caused by unequal talents that luck egalitarianism fails to capture, even if the luck egalitarian distribution is implemented.

There are at least two ways in which relational inequalities may arise from unequal talents, and I will discuss each in turn; through (i) the way in which talents are identified, and (ii) the act of institutions acting on and expressing differences in levels of talent. This list need not be exhaustive for the relational egalitarian's account of talent and inequality to hold. However, in the next section I will argue that the luck egalitarian can also accommodate for these kinds of relational inequalities within their theory, sometimes more successfully than relational egalitarianism.

5.4.1. Talent Identification

To organise a society in a way that takes account of people's different levels of talent, and the way in which those talents give rise to unequal advantages, we would be required to differentiate between those who are talented and those who are not. However, this process of identification may give rise to relational inequalities in the way that it requires those who are untalented to 'reveal' themselves or be 'revealed' (Wolff 1998). This kind of revelation can occur in two ways. First, if those who considered themselves to be unfairly disadvantaged due to their lack of talent wanted compensation or help to overcome the disadvantage, they might be required to reveal their lack of talent and prove that they really are untalented and disadvantaged. Second, if the state needs to assess levels of talent, for education or health reasons for example, comparisons would need to be made that brought out and revealed differences in ability.

Being revealed or having to reveal oneself as untalented has potentially hurtful and humiliating effects for the untalented person, damaging their self-esteem and sense of worth, which in turn may lead to feelings of inferiority. As Wolff claims, "where a particular trait is valued within an agent's culture, to admit that one does not have it can lead one to believe that one will, as a consequence, acquire a lower respect-standing" (Wolff: 110). Anderson similarly argues that relying on the requirement to distinguish a person's level of talent when measuring levels of disadvantage is intrusive and insulting, because it "makes the basis of citizens' claims on one another the fact that some are inferior to others in the worth of their lives, talents, and personal qualities" (Anderson 1999: 289).[53]

Feelings of inferiority, such as a lack of self-respect and self-worth, are considered as highly problematic from the standpoint of relational equality. This is because these emotions play an important part in the way that people gain confidence with regards to their standing in society, and this in turn influences the way that people conduct themselves as equal members of society; Rawls, for example, considered self-respect as the "most important" primary social good

---

[53] Similarly to Wolff and Anderson, Ian Carter has argued that evaluating people's varying levels of talent in the political sphere is disrespectful and unnecessarily delves into a person's personal and private life. However, Carter explicitly claims that the internal evaluation in question is only disrespectful with regards to determining how we treat people as *political* agents. He does admit that when it comes to more substantial "thick" human relationships, such as the one between professor and student, treating people at an evaluative distance "will often be an inappropriate attitude". It is not incoherent, then, for the professor to assess a student's academic ability, but refrain from doing so when treating her as a mutual political agent (Carter: 557). This may be true, but if it is, then there arises a tension when it comes to deciding what to do with regards to talented people in an institutional setting. In one respect we have to ask people to reveal their levels of ability in order to determine what resources will best enable them to flourish, but at the same time, policy decisions about the distribution of resources for talented people are made at the level of impartial, political institutions. It would be interesting to determine whether this tension is damaging for Carter's view, and the extent to which considering people as 'thin' political agents is compatible with the relational egalitarian project of ensuring that people are treated as equals.

(Rawls 1999: 386). As a result, any state of affairs that damages a person's self-worth has the potential to hinder their ability to equally participate as a worthwhile member of society, harming civic friendship and social trust (Fourie: 87, 95). These negative emotions may not arise in every individual who is revealed as 'untalented', or it might be the case that an individual's feelings of inferiority are considered to be irrational. However, as Wolff asserts, "[e]ven if there is no good reason why a particular trait should lower your respect-standing, the fact is that it can, or, at least, may lead one to believe that it will. So even if a source of shame is contingent and irrational, it can still be experienced as a source of shame" (Wolff: 115). And this shame, if it does arise, will result in relational inequalities, rather than inequalities in individual levels of advantage.

Because the inequalities that arise from the identification of talents is relational, in order to counteract these inequalities the relational egalitarian will suggest that instead of assessing whether a person's talent is a result of bad brute luck and re-organising resources to compensate for any personal disadvantages that arise, we ought instead to organise society in such a way that respects each person's level of ability and the various social roles we adopt.[54]

5.4.2. Expressive Acts

It is not only the act of talent identification itself that might cause relational inequalities, but also the expressive act of institutions publically proclaiming differences in levels of talent. This expressive act could correlate to distributive concerns whereby an institution might publically declare that a talented person is more worthy of resources, or more deserving of the power to control shares of resources in society than an untalented person. Although this expressive act and the distributive act will be closely related, and perhaps occur simultaneously, they are distinct. Being told by the state that you are less worthy of resources does not guarantee that you will actually receive less resources or opportunities, or

---

[54] Michael Slote, for example, offers his own way in which to avoid relational inequalities that arise from the identification of talents. He recommends implementing his care ethical approach to moral education in order to increase levels of empathy in students (Slote 2010). As another example, Fishkin recommends that we widen opportunities and lessen the effects of debilitating and unnecessary stop-gaps in society that limit a person's development and set of opportunities (Fishkin 2014).

actually have less power to control those resources. Furthermore, it may be possible for those who are talented to receive an extra distribution of resources, or the power to control those resources, without the fact that they are identified as 'talented' being expressed in public.

The expressive act could also correlate with concerns about talent identification, whereby an institution might publically express that a talented person's level of ability has been identified as superior to an untalented person's level of ability. The declaration of such an identification officially and publically exposes people's comparative level of talent, which means that not only does the untalented person lack self-worth, but that the state also expresses their belief that the untalented person's lack of talent renders them less valuable to the productive functioning of society.

Additionally, the state does not need to *explicitly* express their judgements for feelings of inferiority to occur. Redistribution and identification itself can be interpreted as an implicit act of expression that is just as worrying for the relational egalitarian. All that needs to be in place for relational inequalities to arises is a social structure that makes room for the state to endorse certain social norms underlying the encouragement of unequal power relations. The reasons for the state's actions would be acknowledged and internalised by citizens as legitimate forms of behaviour, and as such, it is the "general knowledge" of the way social institutions act and the way in which they make their judgements that would be particularly demoralising (Anderson 1999: 306; Garrau & Laborde: 60). These expressive acts, whether they are explicit or implicit, can be seen as a state's social failure to treat citizens with equal concern and respect, singling out a certain group of people as less valuable and inferior just in virtue of their level of talent (Anderson 1999: 305-6; Fourie: 101; Slote: 15).

These two examples of how relational inequalities can emerge due to unequal levels of talent are used by relational egalitarians to argue that luck egalitarianism's reliance on bad brute luck is implausible when determining how unequal talents disrupt levels of equality. This is because doing so fails to comprehensively accommodate for *all* arising inequalities that are deemed to be unjust, specifically relational ones. In the next section I will demonstrate that in fact luck egalitarianism can accommodate for these relational inequalities, and in a way that more successfully understands the reasons why inequalities in talent matter to us. As I will argue, this means that luck egalitarianism provides a more successful account of how to counteract unequal levels of talent.

5.5. Relational Inequalities and Luck Egalitarianism

For sake of argument I will not object to the fact that unequal talents can cause the relational inequalities discussed in the two examples above. However, assuming that these relational inequalities do arise from unequal levels of talent, relational egalitarians claim that luck egalitarians cannot successfully capture these inequalities as part of their account of egalitarian justice. As a result, this would mean that luck egalitarianism does not offer a plausible account of how unequal talents disrupt levels of equality.

However, I argue that luck egalitarianism is adequately equipped to accommodate for relational inequalities. Whilst it is the case that relational goods occur interpersonally, this does not mean that they are neglected by a consideration of how to distribute resources in a way that aims to eradicate comparative disadvantages arising because of bad brute luck. The most attractive versions of luck egalitarianism are committed to correcting relational inequalities insofar as they affect levels of comparative advantage, understood personally *and* interpersonally. Cohen, for example, considers the currency of equality (that is, what we are aiming to equalise) to be "access to advantage", where advantage is a broad notion that includes, among other things, a person's level of welfare, personal capacities, material wealth and interpersonal relationships with others (Cohen 2011: 13-14).

Cohen's account of luck egalitarianism makes room for the fact that a person's access to advantage can be disrupted by unequal standings with others in society and by being part of certain kinds of relationships. If someone is made to feel inferior by the revelation that they are untalented, and as a result are marginalised or dominated by others, then this has the potential to put them at a disadvantage, or indeed constitute a disadvantage in itself that arises due to bad brute luck, at least in part. In this way, luck egalitarians *should* be concerned with levels of relational equality – those accounts of luck egalitarianism that do not accommodate for this are implausible.

Furthermore, it seems as if luck egalitarianism can accommodate for relational inequalities caused by unequal talents more successfully than relational egalitarianism itself. This is evident when determining how the two theories assess what counts as an unjust talent inequality, and why talents are valuable to us in the first place. On the one hand, relational egalitarians consider talent inequalities to be unjust only if they affect a person's ability to interact as an equal in society. As Anderson states, "the proper egalitarian aim is to ensure, to the extent feasible, that everyone has sufficient capital to function as an equal in civil society – to avoid oppression by others, to enjoy standing as an equal, to participate in productive life, and so forth" (Anderson 2007: 618). For example, if someone feels inferior due to their low level of talent, this is only problematic if it affects their ability to interact in society as an equal citizen; not all instances of inferiority will have this effect. In fact, Anderson argues that relational egalitarianism will often find "no injustice" with regards to feelings of admiration and inferiority that may come with unequal levels of talents, due to the fact that "one doesn't need to be admired to be able to function as an equal citizen" (Anderson 2010: 335).

On the other hand, luck egalitarianism considers inequalities of relational goods to be unjust if they hinder one's access to advantage and give rise to a comparative disadvantage. In this way, if someone is comparatively disadvantaged as a result of the inferiority that is caused by one's low level of talent, then the luck egalitarian will consider the part of this disadvantage caused by bad brute luck to be unjust. And what counts as an advantage and disadvantage is determined by what is valuable and matters to us.

Therefore, the difference between relational and luck egalitarianism is that when it comes to talent inequalities, they matter for the former only insofar as they hinder relational equality, whereas they matter for luck egalitarianism insofar as they comparatively disadvantage someone with regards to something that matters and is valuable *simpliciter*, even if it does not disrupt relational equality as prescribed by relational egalitarianism (Mason: 219). As such, the luck egalitarian can, in theory, accommodate relational goods more comprehensively than the relational egalitarian, who focuses merely on their own benchmark of what counts as relational equality in terms of equal participation and respect, rather on value and disadvantage more broadly. If the equality of relational goods is valuable, then the luck egalitarian will include it as part of the commitments of their theory.

It is one thing for the luck egalitarian to successfully argue that relational goods *can* be incorporated into their theory of justice. It is another thing altogether, however, for the luck egalitarian to be able to successfully account for *how* they might counteract the inequalities that arise from these relational goods. Luck egalitarianism has been objected to on the basis that it is concerned merely with distributing material goods. If this was the case, then it is unclear how we would be able to 'distribute' relational goods such as self-respect and power relations – these are the kinds of goods that cannot be materially quantified and individually held.

However, there is nothing in luck egalitarianism that prevents it from counteracting relational inequalities that arise from unequal talents in the same way that relational egalitarians would. For example, Chiara Cordelli has proposed that even if we cannot distribute and measure levels of relational goods themselves, we can distribute the *social bases* of these goods (Cordelli: 100; see also Baker: 68). The idea of a 'social basis' refers to Rawls's account of the "features of the basic structure that may reasonably be expected to affect people's self-respect" (Rawls 1999: 254-266). Ensuring that people have equal access to the parts of society that affect someone's self-respect, for example, might include distributing material goods so that each person has enough wealth in order to feel secure, but it might also include reforming moral education to ensure that people are taught to respect and value each other despite their differences. It might also include some other kind of social re-structuring, perhaps changing the way in which talents are identified or resource allocations handed out (see Hirose & Segall: 22; Tan: 104, 130).

Anderson claims that relational egalitarians would prefer to alter social structures and norms rather than redistribute material resources (Anderson: 336), there is, however, nothing to prevent the luck egalitarian from also opting for this relational mode of social restructuring, if indeed it was shown to most effectively and productively counteract arising unjust inequalities. In fact, when it comes to counteracting relational inequalities, the luck egalitarian and the relational egalitarian are left with the same options; there is nothing that egalitarians of any variety can do apart from restructure, reform or redistribute the social bases of these relational goods. For example, Anderson claims that in order to achieve relational equality, the relational egalitarian "requires that each person have sufficient internal capacities and external resources to enjoy security against oppression" and that "each person have enough to function as an equal in society" (Anderson 2007: 620). But luck egalitarianism would require this too, given that a person's oppression and unequal position in society would count as a comparative disadvantage. Even though relational inequalities are innately relational rather than an individual disadvantage, and given the way that society is structured, attending to the social bases of how people treat each other is the only way to socially mitigate for these inequalities (Fishkin: 131-156).

Therefore, even though unequal levels of talent in society may cause relational inequalities, this does not mean that relational egalitarianism is the only or most successful theory to correctly capture the reasons why these relational inequalities are unjust, and how they should be counteracted. Instead, luck egalitarianism is able to accommodate for the worry of relational inequalities caused by unequal talents, and is also able to suggest ways in which to counteract for these relational disadvantages. In the next section I argue that luck egalitarianism is able to offer an account of how to counteract unjust inequalities of talent that is more successful than relational egalitarianism. This is because luck egalitarianism more plausibly understands they reasons why talents are valuable and why unequal talents disrupt levels of equality.[55]

---

[55] Anderson has argued that one of the substantial demarcations between luck and relational egalitarianism is that the focus on social equality for the latter means that what we owe each other depends on interpersonal justification (Anderson 2010; see also Tan: 97). This means that something can only count as a disadvantage for an agent if she

5.6. How to Counteract Unequal Talents

5.6.1. Talents and Opportunity

Unequal levels of talent in society do not only cause relational inequalities. Even if everyone is able to relate to each other and function as equals in society, we still have good reason to be concerned about the unequal levels of talent that remain. This is because the unequal levels of talent that are left over still matter; we value talents not only because they allow us to interact as equals in a participatory society, but because, as I explained in Section Two, talents also give us opportunities for advantage more broadly construed. One of these advantages might very well be the opportunity to interact in society as an equal citizen; developing one's talents may allow us to use a particular skill that can aid one in playing an important and valued role in society. Another advantage of being talented might also be the opportunity for material wealth, with excellent skill acquisition for particular skills often being rewarded by society through economic means.

---

can reasonably make a claim of injustice that others will accept as legitimate (Anderson 2010: 5). In light of this, Anderson writes that "if God does not exist, then there is no one accountable for the unequal distribution of natural endowments, no injury from this, and hence no injustice" (Anderson 2010: 10). There is no injustice, Anderson argues, because there can be no reasonable claim of injustice made on others. However, assuming that interpersonal justification of justice claims are necessary for a theory of egalitarian justice (and we should not automatically accept that they are), it is not clear why luck egalitarianism cannot accommodate this. There is someone whose interests have been hurt, they are disadvantaged, and there is someone or an institution that they can hold accountable for this disadvantage due to the failure in "preventing or remedying the injury" (Anderson 2010: 9). We do not expect the disadvantaged untalented person to ask for the talented pianist's arm to be chopped off so as to equalise their levels of talent, as Anderson suggests. But we would expect them to complain about the fact that their social environment was not structured so as to either (a) give them the opportunity to develop musical talents that they may have but are so far neglected, unidentified or undeveloped, or (b) engender the right kind of conditions for a talent to emerge in the first place. In this way, this person's claim is justifiable in terms of the interpersonal commitments and obligations that we owe to each other – there is no reason why luck egalitarianism cannot accommodate this.

However, the advantages that come with being talented are not exhausted by relational or material instrumental benefits. Being talented is also valuable because of the non-instrumental developmental opportunities it can bestow upon an individual. And, as I have argued in Chapter Three, this developmental experience can uniquely contribute to one's well-being, with the potential to shape one's deeply held commitments and convictions about the good life. Because society is structured to give further developmental opportunities to those who are talented, and provides the environment for certain talents to emerge in the first place, merely having a talent means that you have already been advantaged with a greater opportunity set; this impacts on your life prospects and alters your level of access to advantage. The mere fact that there is an unequal level of talent in society is in part a result of your brute luck in the way that social institutions are structured.

Therefore, we also worry about unequal levels of talent because talents widen a person's opportunity set with regards to one of the most fundamentally important aspects of a person's life – the opportunity for one's own personal development. Because talents are non-instrumentally valuable in this way, as an opportunity for all kinds of advantages, including the opportunity for development, this means that the mere fact that one is not talented counts as a disadvantage; it reduces one's set of advantageous opportunities. As such, luck egalitarians aim to counteract comparative levels of unequal talents in themselves, to the extent that the unequal levels of talent have been caused by bad brute luck, irrespective of the arising disadvantageous or advantageous consequences of this inequality (Segall: 20; Schwartz: 253-7).

By contrast, relational egalitarians claim that unequal differences in talent are not worrying because we value them as advantageous opportunities, but only if they disrupt relational equality. The reason relational egalitarians do not consider the value of talents to matter non-instrumentally for egalitarian justice in and of itself can be traced back to Rawls's claim, that what matters for justice is "the way the basic structure of society makes use of these natural differences and permits them to affect the social fortune of citizens, their opportunities in life, and the actual terms of cooperation between them" (Rawls, 1999: 337; Anderson 1999: 336; see also Tan: 92, 103). On Rawls's picture, talents are considered 'natural' endowments, and inequalities in talent are only unjust with regards to how social institutions *respond* to these natural inequalities, rather than the fact that *there are* unequal levels of talents themselves. This means that the unequal distribution of talents is normatively neutral; we should only aim to counteract the disadvantageous *consequences* of the inequalities that arise as a result of unequal levels of talent, rather than counteract the unequal levels of talent by themselves, as the luck egalitarian proposes.

Luck egalitarians do admit that there are some cases in which natural facts are normatively neutral in the way that relational egalitarians suggest. As Cohen states, "[l]uck might cause one person to have more freckles than another: that is (in itself) neither an equality nor an inequality" (Cohen 2011: 117). But talents are different to freckles in one important respect: we *value* talents for the way in which they can advantageously affect a person's life. That is, the reality of unequal talents is not normatively neutral because they matter to us. And the reason talents matters to us and why we find unequal levels of talent worrying, is not merely because of the instrumental advantages of developing our talents, or the fact that talents can disrupt relational equality. Talents are valuable also due to the non-instrumental value that being talented bestows on us – talents determine a person's advantageous developmental experience.

Furthermore, as I have already argued in Chapter One, talents are not 'natural' as Rawls and most other egalitarians suggest. Instead, they emerge as a dynamic interaction between one's social and natural environment. This means that one's level of talent is in part defined by the social structures and opportunities that are in place in one's society, and already an indication of one's level of social advantage. As a result, someone who is untalented will always be worse off in terms of opportunities than someone who is talented, and will always be worse off than they might otherwise have been, all other things being equal (Segall: 75, 81).[56] The mere fact that there are unequal levels of talent in society

---

[56] This is why Nozick's entitlement theory does not work when it comes to the equal distribution of talents and their development. The entitlement theory that Nozick's Wilt Chamberlain example is meant to illustrate is not persuasive as an account of how distributive justice should deal with the problem of unequal talents, because it assumes a normatively neutral position regarding the status quo and starting point with regards to

demonstrates that there are unjust levels of inequalities that ought to be counteracted; merely having a comparatively lower level of talent disadvantages and limits one's access to valuable opportunities, and this disadvantage occurs, at least in part, as a result of both natural and social brute luck. Therefore, it is the luck egalitarian, and not the relational egalitarian, that successfully understands the way in which we ought to respond to unequal talents. The luck egalitarian claims that insofar as one's level of talent is matter of bad brute luck, we ought to counteract the unequal levels of talent in themselves and not just the disadvantageous consequences that arise due to these unequal levels of talent.

5.6.2. Mitigation and Neutralisation

Given the fact that we also value talents non-instrumentally, as an advantage for all kinds of opportunities, the luck egalitarian further claims that we should not only *mitigate* the disadvantageous effects of unequal talents, but that we ought to *neutralise* the unjust inequalities in the distribution of talents itself. As Cohen claims, "the fundamental egalitarian aim is to *extinguish* the influence of brute luck on distribution" (Cohen 2011: 391, see also Tan: 127). This luck egalitarian neutralisation approach considers the level of one's talent to be valuable simpliciter, and so aims to neutralise any unjust inequalities in levels of talent before they arise.[57]

---

people's talents and abilities. Chamberlain is allowed to keep his higher earnings because people are free and able to pay to see him perform, so the problem of material inequalities is not unjust in this situation, according to Nozick. However, as we know, the emergence of Chamberlain's talent is in part a result of bad brute luck. This means that Chamberlain's talent has advantaged him unfairly. Chamberlain is not necessarily 'entitled' to his talent, even if he is entitled to the fruits of his talent. When on a level playing field, people would be entitled to any success that arises from their effort to develop their talent; but we are not on a level playing field. The truth is that Chamberlain's talent is the result of unfair social and natural advantages, and so even if people freely chose to give him money, we ought to find a way to make the social structure fairer, *before* the question of redistribution arises (see Nozick 1974).

[57] Note that luck egalitarianism is concerned with neutralising the *disadvantageous effects* of luck and not neutralising luck itself. This is important, as the bad effects of one instance of luck can plausibly be eliminated by another. Luck merely triggers the luck egalitarian concern that something is potentially unjust, and it is the comparative disadvantage caused by that luck that signals the injustice.

By contrast, relational egalitarians merely aim to *mitigate* the negative effects of unequal talents, rather than completely neutralising the unjust level of inequality in the first place. This means that some differences in levels of talent are allowed to remain, insofar as these differences do not unreasonably hinder a person's access to relational equality (Mason: 10, 94). As Anderson states, inequalities are only considered to be unjust by relational egalitarians when the inequality "reflects, embodies, or causes inequality of authority, status or standing" (Anderson 2010: 2). Once these criteria have been met, however, relational egalitarians do not worry about unequal levels of talent. In fact, at times it seems that Anderson doubts altogether whether unequal talents really do disrupt relational equality, and as such, the inequalities that arise from differential talents would not be deemed as unjust, and so would not need to be mitigated (Anderson 2007: 620).

The difference between the relational egalitarian's mitigation approach, and the luck egalitarian's neutralisation approach can be summarised as follows: the mitigation approach considers the disadvantageous effects of unequal talents as unjust, after the distribution of talents has already occurred (*ex post*), whereas the neutralisation approach considers the mere fact of an unequal distribution of talents to be unjust in itself (to the extent that it arises due to bad brute luck), and aims to counteract this injustice before it arises (*ex ante*).

I argue that we ought to adopt the luck egalitarian's neutralisation approach, because the mitigation approach does not successfully account for how to compensate for the deficiency of opportunities that are lost through a lack of talent (see Dworkin 2013: 359). If someone is not talented, it is not only compensation for the lack of instrumental resources or relational goods that they require, but also compensation for the non-instrumental disadvantage accrued due to the lack of developmental opportunities – for not being the kind of person who is given the various developmental and educational experiences that come with being talented. We want our account of how to counteract unequal talents to accommodate the value of these developmental opportunities, because the value that is received from one's formative developmental experiences turn us into the people that we are.

However, the mitigation approach only counteracts the negative effects of a lack of talent after the fact, and leaves the actual unequal distribution of talents intact. This is unattractive, because we cannot merely compensate for or remediate a lack of developmental experiences after the fact. This is because we value the developmental process not just for the arising beneficial consequences, but also for the experience of the formative process in and of itself. It is this experience that shapes who we are and the values that we hold. If we merely mitigate for this after the fact, then the developmental experience itself will be lost and the disadvantages arising from this left untouched (Fishkin: 22). Therefore, we ought not to merely mitigate *ex post* for the arising disadvantages caused by unequal talents, but to adopt the luck egalitarian approach of neutralising the unjust talent inequalities in themselves.

There are two objections that can be brought against the neutralisation approach. First, it can be argued that neutralisation is impractical, and that we will never be able to successfully eradicate differences in unequal talents before they occur. For example, in order to neutralise differences in musical ability, we might be required to chop off the fingers of those who are talented or carry out invasive brain surgery (Mason: 98). However, to begin with, this objection assumes that in order to neutralise we would have to level down, reducing everyone's level of talent to the lowest common denominator. However, there is nothing to say that we ought to do this, and the most attractive account of neutralisation will level up rather than level down, so that developmental opportunities and experiences are in fact widened for everyone (see for example Fishkin 2014). Furthermore, the objection misunderstands the commitments of egalitarian justice, which determine only what we are required to do in terms of equality, not what should be done all-things-considered. In other words, equality is only thought of as one value that can be trumped by others, and what we ought to do in the name of equality need only be *pro tanto*. In this way, the requirement of neutralisation is only *pro tanto*; it does not specify what we ought to do all-things-considered and can be overridden by other reasons that appeal to some important values (Cohen 2003: 244).[58]

Second, Mason argues that the neutralisation approach results in counter-intuitive implications, claiming that it "is so at odds with our ordinary moral experience" that we should reject it "from the point of view of justice" (Mason: 99, 105). He uses the example of parents choosing to read bedtime stories to their children, which can be seen to advantage children significantly, and consequently cause unjust inequalities in developmental opportunities and experiences. If we follow the luck egalitarian neutralisation approach, then we would have to ensure that any advantages arising from this activity were completely eradicated before they occurred, presumably by requiring parents to refrain from reading to their children in the first place. The point is that if the neutralisation approach were correct, then there would be a *pro tanto* reason of justice to ask parents not to read bedtime stories to their children. Mason claims that this is an unattractive consequence of the neutralisation approach, and goes against what common-sense justice would demand (Mason: 101).

However, in support of the neutralisation approach, Mason's claim can be responded to in two ways. First, as already highlighted above, just because there is a reason not to read to our children in the name of egalitarian justice, this does not mean that, all-things-considered, there aren't other values that might trump this *pro tanto* reason, such as the fostering of intimate relations between parent and child (Brighouse & Swift: 120). This overriding reason, whatever it might be, does not however negate the *pro tanto* reason of equality. Instead, all it demonstrates is that equality is not the only value that we ought to consider when weighing up what should be done overall, and it certainly does not mean we should reject the aim of equality altogether.

Second, Mason's objection can be responded to by highlighting why we value bedtime reading. Bedtime stories are valuable not just because they will bring advantageous benefits to one's children after the experience is over, but

---

[58] Of course, it is another matter what counts as a value that can legitimately trump equality, and how to distinguish what we ought to do overall given these competing values.

also because of the non-instrumental goodness of the experience itself at the time. By mitigating the negative effects of that experience, as Mason suggests we should, we would only be counteracting for the arising unequal consequences. This, however, fails to account for the non-instrumental reasons why we value the opportunity and experience itself. As such, we ought to neutralise and eradicate the mere fact that some children are being read to at bedtime and some are not; this does not necessarily require levelling down, so that we ought to refrain completely from all bedtime reading, but would more plausibly require that social structures are in place so that all children could benefit from such a positive experience.

There will, however, be some cases in which *ex ante* neutralisation is not possible, in part because there will always be an element of natural luck involved in talent formation that social re-structuring cannot counteract, and in part because there are other values, such as autonomy, self-entitlement, efficiency, and family partiality, that will always disrupt levels of equality in talents and their development. Even though there will still be *ex post* inequalities in the levels of talent, I argue that the luck egalitarian neutralisation approach is still the best way to counteract for these inequalities. This is because the fact that there are *ex post* inequalities in talents means that there is a comparative disadvantage in someone's access to advantage, and this disadvantage was in part caused by bad brute luck. Once it has been determined that these inequalities are unjust, then there is no reason to merely mitigate the disadvantageous effects of these inequalities. As I have already argued, this would fail to recognise the non-instrumental value of talent and the experiences it offers. Instead, if someone is comparatively disadvantaged due to their level of talent – whether this disadvantage is relational, material, or developmental – then as egalitarians we ought to aim to eradicate the inequality in the level of talents altogether, both *ex ante* and *ex post*.

Therefore, egalitarian justice demands that we counteract arising inequalities in levels of talent through neutralisation. It is luck egalitarianism, rather than relational egalitarianism, that has the resources to successfully capture this demand, due to the fact that luck egalitarians give a more inclusive account regarding the reasons why we value talents and the advantages that occur from them.

5.7. Conclusion

In this chapter I have argued that when it comes to the relationship between unequal talents and egalitarian justice, it is the theory of luck egalitarianism that is most successful in (a) accounting for why inequalities in talents are considered to be unjust, and (b) prescribing the correct way in which we ought to counteract these inequalities, through neutralisation. Whilst relational egalitarianism has been important in picking out the ways in which unjust relational inequalities can arise from unequal talents, it is not the case that luck egalitarianism cannot accommodate for these. In fact, when it comes to unequal talents it seems as if luck egalitarianism is more comprehensive in addressing these relational inequalities. Furthermore, given the fact that talents emerge in part due to advantageous social structures, it is not the case that talents are by themselves normatively neutral. The mere fact that there are unequal levels of talent distributed in society means that there has already been an instance of unequal social structures.

However, Lippert-Rasmussen argues that the correct account of egalitarian justice ought to be *pluralist*, including commitments held by *both* luck and relational egalitarianism. He writes that "pluralist egalitarians think that luck and relational egalitarians each articulate a component in a pluralistic account of egalitarian justice", and in this pluralistic conception both components "must be satisfied in order for egalitarian justice to fully obtain" (Lippert-Rasmussen 2005: 220-1). The luck egalitarian component would claim that a "state of affairs where people's distributive positions reflect something other than their comparative exercise of responsibility is unjust", whilst the relational component would state that "a just society is one where the norms regulating social interactions are suitably egalitarian, universally accepted and complied with" (Lippert-Rasmussen 2015: 222; see also Voorhoeve: 5).

As I have made explicit in this chapter, it is not clear why relational egalitarianism has the monopoly over the second component that Lippert-Rasmussen mentions, regarding equal social norms and interactions. Luck egalitarians can also accommodate the claim that society ought to be structured in a way that secures the equality of relational goods in insofar as these goods will count as advantages. I have also argued that if we accept a decent and attractive theory of luck egalitarianism, that theory can accommodate the relational inequalities that arise from unequal talents, and provide a more convincing account of how we ought to neutralise any injustice that may arise from these inequalities. As a result, we do not need to be relational egalitarians or pluralist about egalitarian justice when it comes to the relationship between talent and equality; luck egalitarianism can capture everything that relational egalitarianism has told us is unjust about unequal talents, and do so more successfully. Therefore, the way in which we ought to counteract for unequal talents is best understood by referring to the theory of luck egalitarianism, which advocates a neutralisation approach that is successfully grounded in a plausible account of why we value talents and their development and how they disrupt levels of equality.

Conclusion

In this dissertation I have offered an analysis of the nature and value of talent by focussing on three central issues that arise when examining the role that talents play in our lives. To begin with, I focussed on proposing an account of the nature of talent. In Chapter One I argued that a talent is a high level of potential for a particular skill which is expressed in the excellent acquisition of that skill. By making a case for understanding potential as a dispositional quality that results from a dynamic interaction between one's genetic code and one's environment, I objected to the environmentalist account of talent. I then proposed that a talent is an expressive and comparative phenomenon, dependent on the evaluative judgements regarding the value of the skill itself and the various thresholds of comparison classes.

Second, I focussed on whether or not we have good prudential reasons or a moral obligation to develop our talents. In Chapter Two I concentrated on the relationship between talent development and morality, analysing Kant's claim that there is a positive, imperfect moral duty to develop one's talents. I argued that Kant is unsuccessful in providing plausible arguments for this claim, because he cannot generate the moral priority of developing one's talents over one's mere competencies or non-talent abilities.

In Chapter Three I argued that moral perfectionism is similarly unable to generate the claim that there is a moral obligation to develop one's talents. This is because moral perfectionism is subject to what I call the 'excellence objection', showing that developing one's talents is not objectively good or excellent in the way that moral perfectionists advocate. I also argued in Chapter Three that welfare perfectionists cannot successfully claim that there are good prudential reasons to develop one's talents. Not only is welfare perfectionism also subject to the excellence objection, but it also violates the endorsement constraint. This constraint claims that whether or not the development of one's talents is to be regarded as a constituent part of an agent's well-being is conditional on the agent's endorsement of that development, under optimal decision-making conditions. This endorsement appeals to the fit between an agent's deeply held normative commitments and the commitments that are required to bring about the development of her talents. Without this endorsement, the development of one's talents will be alienating, and thus cannot be prudentially good. As such, the endorsement constraint places conditions on any theory of well-being that claims one has a *pro tanto* prudential reason to develop one's talents.

In Chapter Four I argued that the endorsement constraint does not only place conditions on theories of well-being, but also on any moral theory that claims one has a *pro tanto* moral obligation to develop one's talents. Without an agent's endorsement, as specified by the endorsement constraint, the obligation to develop one's talents will count as unreasonably demanding and thus can be overridden by one's deeply held normative commitments. This means that whether or not one has a *pro tanto* prudential reason or a *pro tatno* moral obligation to develop one's talents, will be conditional on meeting the endorsement constraint.

Finally, I turned my focus to the relationship between talent and equality, and what we ought to do given the fact of unequal talents. I argued that luck egalitarianism, rather than relational egalitarianism, most successfully (a) accounts for why inequalities in talent matter for egalitarian justice and should be considered as unjust, and (b) prescribes the way in which we ought to counteract inequalities in levels of talent, through neutralisation, both *ex ante* and *ex post*.

For reasons of scope, I have had to leave some interesting questions unanswered, and these questions highlight potential avenues for further research. With regards to my discussion of the nature of talent in Chapter One, I had to leave aside the issue of how my own account of talent, which answered the conceptual question about what a talent is, fits with what Sternberg and Davidson call 'explicit' theories of talent. This latter type of theory aims to understand the cognitive traits and processes that are present in a person who is already labelled as being talented (Sternberg & Davidson 1986: 10). In order to offer a fully comprehensive account of the nature of talent, it will be important to analyse more extensively the way in which those who are talented use certain cognitive traits and processes to express the excellent manifestation of their skill. For example, Renzulli offers his "three-ring" conception of talent, claiming that talented individuals show a higher level of ability, creativity, and task development (Renzulli 2005). In order to determine which explicit theory is most plausible, more empirical work will need to be undertaken, as well as a theoretical analysis of what is meant by the concepts being used to describe these epistemic and cognitive attributes.

When it came to my discussion of how talent development contributes to one's well-being, in Chapter Three I employed the endorsement constraint to argue that whether or not talent development is prudentially good depends on whether or not an agent endorses (under optimal decision-making conditions) the commitments that are required to bring about the development of her talent. In order to avoid the 'correctness objection', I included as part of this constraint a counter-factual idealisation clause, highlighting that the prudential goodness of talent development does not just rest on an agent's endorsement *simpliciter*, but on what an agent *would* endorse if she were under optimal decision-making conditions.

However, when arguing for this counter-factual clause, I admitted that there was a burden of proof to specify what these optimal conditions are, and how they differ from full idealisation conditions in a way that is not problematically vague or *ad hoc*. As such, it will be important to undertake further research into articulating an account of counter-factual optimal conditions for the endorsement constraint that does not give rise to the objections raised against full idealisation conditions. One way in which to approach formulating such an account will be to examine the literature on decision theory and the extent to which these theories are plausibly applicable to decisions about endorsement and well-being (see for example Peterson 2017).

In Chapter Four, I had to leave aside the question of the role that endorsement plays when determining what is morally required of us in emergency situations, such as in war-time, in the face of humanitarian crises, or in severe health epidemics. In these situations it is thought that what is legitimely required of us by morality will be more extreme and demanding, given the circumstances. In order to provide a comprehensive account of the extent to which talent development is morally required, it will be important to examine in more detail the relationship between endorsement and emergency morality. It might be the case that the endorsement constraint only kicks in after a certain normative humanitarian threshold is met, in which case, we might have a moral obligation to develop talents that we don't endorse. However, if this were true, then where that threshold lies and what counts as 'emergency' morality would need to be plausibly determined (see for example Viens & Selgelid 2012).

Another topic for further research would be an analysis of whether the development of one's talents is morally required not just in secular morality, but also in religious accounts of morality. For example, in Christian ethics, the *Parable of the Talents*, as it appears in the books of Matthew and Luke, seems to suggest that developing one's talents is morally required, given that one's talents are a gift from God. Presumably, given that such an obligation will be a result of divine command, appeal to the endorsement constraint will not be relevant in determining the grounds for this moral obligation. However, further research would be required to arrive at a plausible interpretation of the parables, and an account of the way in which the moral obligation to develop one's talents is generated from the relevant religious commitments (see for example Boucher 1981; Crossan 2013; Hultgren 2000; Snodgrass 2008).

Finally, when it comes to the relationship between talent and equality, I argued that in order to counteract the unequal distribution of levels of talent in society, we ought to adopt the luck egalitarian neutralisation approach. For the sake of discussion in that Chapter, I had to leave aside the interesting practical question about how such a neutralisation approach could be appropriated into public policy and put into practice so as to successfully counteract the injustice caused by unequal talents. One obstacle to this that I initially raised was the assumption that neutralisation would require levelling down, so that we reduce all levels of talent to the lowest common denominator. I argued that neutralisation does not require this, and that we could instead level up so that we maximise levels of talent for everyone as far as possible. However, it would be for further research to examine exactly how this levelling up approach would work in practice, and how other competing values that may conflict with what equality requires will limit the extent to which this approach could be fully implemented.

In the Introduction of this dissertation I noted that despite the fact that talents and their development are considered to play a positive and central role in our lives, the philosophical literature is seriously lacking in its discussion on the nature and value of talents. The literature seems to assume that developing one's talents is good, without an analysis of what talents are and of the value of talent development for one's well-being or moral agency. This dissertation aimed to provide such an analysis, and to demonstrate how this can inform and help us to assess some of the arguments made in the existing philosophical literature. In doing so, I did not aim to provide an exhaustive overview of all the philosophical issues that could be raised in relation to talent and talent development. Instead, by focussing on the central issues of morality, well-being and equality, as well providing an account of the nature of talent and outlining a number of areas for future research, I hope to have at least stimulated a philosophical discussion on the nature and value of talent, and the extent to which talents shape the way that we live our lives.

Bibliography

Adams, Robert, *Finite and Infinite Goods: A Framework for Ethics* (New York: Oxford University Press, 2002)

Anderson, Elizabeth, 'What is the Point of Equality?', *Ethics*, Vol. 109, No. 2 (January 1999): 287-337

Anderson, Elizabeth, 'Fair Opportunity in Education: A Democratic Equality Perspective', *Ethics*, Vol. 117, No. 4 (July 2007): 595-622

Anderson, Elizabeth, 'The Fundamental Disagreement between Luck Egalitarians and Relational Egalitarians', *Canadian Journal of Philosophy*, Supplementary Volume 36 (2010): 1-23

Arneson, Richard, 'Equality and Equality of Opportunity for Welfare', *Philosophical Studies*, Vol. 56, No. 1 (May 1989): 77-93

Arneson, Richard, 'Perfectionism and Politics', *Ethics*, Vol. 111, No. 1 (October 2000): 37-63

Arneson, Richard, 'Luck Egalitarianism – A Primer', in Carl Knight and Zosia Stemplowska (eds.), *Responsibility and Distributive Justice* (Oxford University Press 2011): 24-50

Arts Council England (2017), *Our Mission and Strategy*, http://www.artscouncil.org.uk/about-us/our-mission-and-strategy, accessed 30.03.2017

Axelsen, David V., and Bidadanure, Juliana, 'Unequally Egalitarian? Defending the Egalitarian Credentials of Social Egalitarianism', *CRISPP* (forthcoming)

Bagnoli, Carla, 'Practical Necessity and Agential Autonomy: A Kantian Response to Williams' Objection of Misrepresentation', Conference Paper,

Northwestern Ethics Conference (2009), http://www.philosophy.northwestern.edu/community/nustep/09/papers/Bagnoli.pdf, accessed 29.03.17

Baier, Kurt, *The Moral Point of View: A Rational Basis of Ethics* (Ithaca, New York: Cornell University Press, 1958)

Baker, John, 'Conceptions and Dimensions of Social Equality' in Carina Fourie, Fabian Schuppert, and Ivo Wallimann-Helmer (eds), *Social Equality: On What it Means to be Equals* (Oxford: Oxford University Press, 2015): 65-86

Beck, S., Olek, A., Walter, J., 'From Genomics to Epigenomics: A Loftier View of Life', *Nature Biotechnology*, Vol. 17, No. 12 (December 1999): 1144

Berkey, Brian, 'The Demandingness of Morality: Toward a Reflective Equilibrium', *Philosophical Studies*, Vol. 173, No. 11 (2016): 3015-3035

Boucher, Madeleine I., *The Parables* (Dublin: Veritas Publications, 1981)

Braddock, Matthew, 'Defusing the Demandingness Objection: Unreliable Intuitions', *Journal of Social Philosophy*, Vol. 44, No. 2 (Summer 2013): 169-191

Bradford, Gwen, 'The Value of Achievements', *Pacific Philosophical Quarterly*, Vol. 94, Issue 2 (June 2013): 204-224

Brandt, Richard B., *Facts, Values and Morality* (Cambridge: Cambridge University Press, 1996)

Brighouse, Harry and Swift, Adam, Equality, 'Priority, and Positional Goods', *Ethics*, Vol. 116, No. 3 (April 2006): 471-497

Brink, David O., 'Prudence and Authenticity: Intrapersonal Conflicts of Value', *The Philosophical Review*, Vol. 112, No. 2 (April, 2003): 215-245

Carbonell, Vanessa, 'Sacrifices of Self', *The Journal of Ethics*, Vol. 19, No. 1 (March, 2015): 53-72

Carter, Ian, 'Respect and the Basis of Equality', *Ethics*, Vol. 121, No. 3 (2011): 538-571

Chang, Ruth, 'The Possibility of Parity', *Ethics*, Vol. 112, No. 4 (July 2002): 659-688

Chang, Ruth, 'Putting Together Morality and Well-Being', in Peter Baumann & Monika Betzler (eds), *Practical Conflicts: New Philosophical Essays* (Cambridge: Cambridge University Press, 2004): 118-158

Chang, Ruth, 'Grounding Practical Normativity: Going Hybrid', *Philosophical Studies*, Vol. 164, No. 1 (2013): 163-187

Chang, Ruth, 'Transformative Choices', *Res Philosophica*, Vol. 92, No.2 (2015): 237-282

Chappell, Timothy, 'Integrity and Demandingness', *Ethical Theory and Moral Practice*, Vol. 10, No. 3 (June 2007): 255-265

Choi, Sungho, 'What is a Dispositional Masker?', *Mind*, Vol. 120, No. 480 (October 2011): 1159-1171

Cohen, G. A., 'Facts and Principles', *Philosophy and Public Affairs*, Vol. 31, Issue 3 (July 2003): 211-245

Cohen, G. A., *The Currency of Egalitarian Justice, and Other Essays in Political Philosophy*, ed. Michael Otsuka (Princeton/Oxford: Princeton University Press, 2011)

Colburn, Ben, *Autonomy and Liberalism* (New York/Oxford: Routledge, 2010)

Colburn, Ben, 'Disadvantage, Autonomy, and the Continuity Test', *Journal of Applied Philosophy*, Vol. 31, No. 3 (2014): 254-270

Colvin, Geoff, *Talent is Overrated* (London/Boston: Nicholas Brealey Publishing Ltd, 2008)

Cordelli, Chiara, 'Justice as Fairness and Relational Resources', *Journal of Political Philosophy*, Vol. 23, Issue 1 (March 2015): 86-110

Cottingham, John, 'Impartiality and Ethical Formation', in Brian Feltham & John Cottingham (eds.), *Partiality and Impartiality: Morality, Special Relationships, and the Wider World* (Oxford: Oxford University Press 2010): 65-83

Coyle, Daniel, *The Talent Code* (London: Random House 2009)

Creative Scotland (2014), *Unlocking Potential, Embracing Ambition: A Shared Plan for Arts, Screen and Creative Industries 2014-2024,* http://www.creativescotland.com/__data/assets/pdf_file/0012/25500/Creative-Scotland-10-Year-Plan-2014-2024-v1-2.pdf, accessed 30.03.17

Crossan, John Dominic, *The Power of Parable: How Fiction by Jesus Became Fiction about Jesus* (New York: HarperCollins Publishers, 2013)

Crisp, Roger, 'Raz on Well-Being' *Oxford Journal of Legal Studies*, Vol. 17, No. 3 (1997): 499-515

Csikszentmihalyi, Mihaly, 'Fruitless Polarities', *Behavioral and Brain Sciences,* Vol. 21, No. 3 (1998): 411

Csikszentmihalyi, Mihaly, *The Systems Model of Creativity: The Collected Works of Mihaly Csikszentmihalyi* (New York: Springer, 2015)

Darwall, Stephen, 'Reasons, Motives, and the Demands of Morality: An Introduction', in Stephen Darwall (ed.), *Moral Discourse and Practice: Some Philosophical Approaches* (Oxford: Oxford University Press, 1997): 305-12

Denis, Lara, 'Kant's Ethics and Duties to Oneself' *Pacific Philosophical Quarterly*, Vol. 78, Issue 4 (December 1997): 321-348

Dorsey, Dale, 'Three Arguments for Perfectionism', *Noûs*, Vol. 4, No. 1 (February 2010): 59-79

Dorsey, Dale, 'Weak Anti-Rationalism and the Demands of Morality', *Noûs*, Vol. 46, No. 1 (February 2012): 1-23

Dworkin, Ronald, *Sovereign Virtue: The Theory and Practice of Equality* (Cambridge, MA: Harvard University Press, 2000)

Dworkin, Ronald, 'Equality, Luck and Hierarchy', *Philosophy and Public Affairs*, Vol. 31, Issue 2 (April 2003): 198-198

Dworkin, Ronald, *Justice for Hedgehogs* (Cambridge, MA: The Belknap Press of Harvard University Press, 2013)

Eckhardt, F., Beck, S., Gut I. G., Berlin, K., 'Future Potential of the Human Epigenome Project', *Expert Review of Molecular Diagnostics*, Vol. 4, No. 5 (September 2004): 609-618

Eisenberg, Paul D., 'Duties to Oneself and the Concept of Morality' *Inquiry*, Vol. 11, Issue 1-4 (1968): 129-154

Enoch, David, 'Why Idealize', *Ethics*, Vol. 115, No. 4 (July, 2005): 759-787

Fairbanks, Sandra Jane, *Kantian Morality and the Destruction of the Self* (Boulder, Colorado: Westview Press, 2000)

Fara, Michael, 'Masked Abilities and Compatibilism', *Mind*, Vol. 17, No. 468 (October 2008): 843-865

Feldman, D. H., 'Giftedness as a Developmentalist Sees It', in Robert J. Sternberg & Janet E. Davidson (eds), *Conceptions of Giftedness* (New York: Cambridge University Press, 1986): 285-305

Ferkany, Matt, 'The Objectivity of Wellbeing', *Pacific Philosophical Quarterly*, Vol. 93, Issue 4 (December 2012): 472-492

Firth, Roderick, 'Ethical Absolutism and the Ideal Observer', *Philosophy and Phenomenological Research,* 12 (1952): 317-345

Fishkin, Joseph, *Bottlenecks: A New Theory of Equal Opportunity* (New York: Oxford University Press, 2014)

Fourie, Carina, 'To Praise and to Scorn: The Problem of Inequalities of Esteem for Social Egalitarianism', in Carina Fourie, Fabian Schuppert, and Ivo Wallimann-Helmer (eds), *Social Equality: On What it Means to be Equals* (Oxford University Press, 2015): 87-106

Gagné, Françoys, 'A Biased Survey and Interpretation of the Nature-Nurture Literature', in *Behavioral and Brain Sciences,* Vol. 21, No. 3 (1998): 415-416

Gagné, Françoys, 'Yes, Giftedness (aka "Innate" Talent) Does Exist!', in Scott Barry Kaufman (ed.), *The Complexity of Greatness: Beyond Talent or Practice* (New York: Oxford University Press, 2013): 191-222

Garrau, Marie & Larborde, Cécile, 'Relational Equality, Non-Domination, and Vulnerability', in Carina Fourie, Fabian Schuppert, and Ivo Wallimann-Helmer (eds), *Social Equality: On What it Means to be Equals* (Oxford University Press, 2015): 45-64

Goodin, Robert E., 'Demandingness as Virtue', *Journal of Ethics,* Vol. 13, No. 1 (2009): 1-13

Green, T. H., *Prolegomena to Ethics*, ed. David O. Brink (Oxford: Oxford University Press, 2003)

Griffin, James, *Well-Being: Its Meaning, Measurement, and Moral Importance* (Oxford: Clarendon Press, 1988)

Handfield, Toby, 'Dispositions, Manifestations, and Causal Structure' in Anna Marmodoro (ed.), *The Metaphysics of Powers: Their Grounding and their Manifestations* (New York: Routledge, 2010)

Haybron, Daniel M., 'Well-being and Virtue', *Journal of Ethics and Social Philosophy*, Vol. 2, No. 2 (August 2007): 1 – 27

Hirose, Iwao & Segall, Shlomi, 'Equality and Political Philosophy' (unpublished manuscript, 2016), https://www.academia.edu/23553375/Equality_and_Political_Philosophy, accessed 21.02.17

Hooker, Brad, 'The Demandingness Objection', in Timothy Chappell (ed.), *The Problem of Moral Demandingness* (London: Palgrave Macmillan, 2009): 148-162

Howe, Michael J. A., Davidson, Jane W., Moore, Derek G., & Sloboda, John A., 'Are There Early Childhood Signs of Musical Ability', *Psychology of Music*, Vol. 23, No. 2 (October 1995): 162-176

Howe, Michael J. A., Davidson, Jane W., & Sloboda, John A., 'Innate Talents: Reality or Myth', *Behavioral and Brain Sciences*, Vol. 21, No. 3 (1998): 399-442

Hultgren, Arland J., *The Parables of Jesus: A Commentary* (Grand Rapids, Michigan/Cambridge, UK: William B. Eerdmans Publishing Company, 2000)

Humboldt, von W., *The Limits of State Action*, ed. J. W. Burrow (New York: Cambridge University Press, 1969)

Hurka, Thomas, *Perfectionism* (New York: Oxford University Press, 1993)

Hurley, Paul, *Beyond Consequentialism* (Oxford: Oxford University Press, 2009)

Hurley, Susan L., 'Debate: Luck, Responsibility, and the 'Natural Lottery', *The Journal of Political Philosophy*, Vol. 10, No. 1 (2002): 79-94

Kagan, Shelly, 'Well-Being as Enjoying the Good', *Philosophical Perspectives*, Vol. 31, Issue 1 (December 2009): 253-272

Kant, *The Metaphysics of Morals*, trans. & ed. Mary Gregor (New York: Cambridge University Press, 1996)

Kant, *Groundwork for the Metaphysics of Morals*, trans. & ed. Mary Gregor (New York: Cambridge University Press, 2010)

Kant, *Anthropology from a Pragmatic Point of View*, trans. & ed. Robert B. Louden (New York: Cambridge University Press, 2006)

Kauppinen, Antti, 'Working Hard and Kicking Back: The Case for Diachronic Perfectionism' *Journal of Ethics and Social Philosophy*, Discussion Note (April 2009): 1-9

Kitcher, Philip, 'Essence and Perfection', *Ethics*, Vol. 110, No. 1 (October 1999): 59-83

Korsgaard, Christine, 'Kant's Formula of the Universal Law', in *Pacific Philosophical Quarterly*, XCHII, No. 2 (April, 1983): 169-195

Korsgaard, Christine, 'Two Distinction in Goodness', *The Philosophical Review*, Vol. 66, No. 1-2 (1985): 24-47

Korsgaard, Christine, *The Sources of Normativity* (Cambridge: Cambridge University Press, 1996)

Korsgaard, Christine, 'Kant's Analysis of Obligation: The Argument of *Groundwork I*' in Paul Guyer (ed.), *Kant's Groundwork of the Metaphysics of Morals: Critical Essays* (Maryland: Rowman & Littlefield Publishers, Inc., 1998): 51-80

Kraut, Richard, *What is Good and Why: The Ethics of Well-Being* (Cambridge, MA: Harvard University Press, 2009)

Knight, Carl, 'Luck Egalitarianism', *Philosophy Compass*, Vol. 8, No. 10 (2013): 924-934

Knight, Carl 'Egalitarian Justice and Valuational Judgement', *Journal of Moral Philosophy*, Vol. 6, No. 4 (2009): 482-498

Kymlicka, Will, *Contemporary Political Philosophy: An Introduction* (Oxford: Clarendon Press: 1990)

Lazenby, Hugh, 'Mistakes and the Continuity Test', *Politics, Philosophy & Economics*, Vol. 15, No. 2 (2016): 190-205

Lippert-Rasmussen, Kasper, 'Hurley on Egalitarianism and the Luck-Neutralizing Aim', *Politics, Philosophy and Economics*, Vol. 4, No. 2 (2005): 249-265

Lippert-Rasmussen, Kasper, 'Luck-Egalitarians versus Relational Egalitarians: On the Prospects of Pluralist account of Egalitarian Justice', *Canadian Journal of Philosophy*, Vol. 45, No. 2 (2015): 220-241

Martin, C. B., 'Dispositions and Conditionals', *The Philosophical Quarterly*, Vol. 44, No. 174 (January 1994): 1-8

Mason, Andrew, *Levelling the Playing Field: The Idea of Equal Opportunity and its Place in Egalitarian Thought* (Oxford: Oxford University Press, 2006)

MacIntrye, Alasdair, *After Virtue* (Notre Dame, Indiana: University of Notre Dame Press, 1984)

McKinsey & Company (2017), *Human Capital*, http://www.mckinsey.com/business-functions/organization/how-we-help-clients/human-capital, accessed 30.03.17

McTernan, Emily, 'How to Be a Responsibility-Sensitive Egalitarian: From Metaphysics to Social Practice', *Political Studies*, Vol. 64, No. 3 (2016): 748-764

Mill, John Stuart, *On Liberty* (Mineola, New York: Dover Publications, Inc., 2002)

Moseley, Daniel D., 'Revisiting Williams on Integrity', *Journal of Value Inquiry*, Vol. 48, No. 1 (March 2014): 53-68

Mumford, Stephen, *Dispositions* (Oxford: Oxford University Press, 1998)

Murphy, Liam B., *Moral Demands and Nonideal Theory* (Oxford: Oxford University Press, 2003)

Nozick, Robert, *Anarchy, State, and Utopia* (Oxford: Basic Books, 1977)

Nussbaum, Martha C., 'Adaptive Preferences and Women's Options', *Economics and Philosophy*, Vol. 17, No. 1 (April 2001): 67-88

O'Neill, Onora, 'Consistency in Action' in Paul Guyer (ed.), *Kant's Groundwork of the Metaphysics of Morals: Critical Essays* (Maryland: Rowman & Littlefield Publishers, Inc., 1998): 103-132

Parfit, Derek, *Reasons and Persons* (Oxford: Oxford University Press, 1984)

Parfit, Derek, *On What Matters: Volume One* (Oxford: Oxford University Press, 2011)

Paton, H. J., *The Categorical Imperative: A Study in Kant's Moral Philosophy* (Philadelphia, Pennsylvania: University of Pennsylvania Press, 1971)

Paton, Margaret, 'A Reconsideration of Kant's Treatment of Duties to Oneself', *The Philosophical Quarterly*, Vol. 40, No. 159 (April, 1990): 222-233

Peterson, Martin, *An Introduction to Decision Theory*, Second Edition (Cambridge: Cambridge University Press, 2017)

Portmore, Douglas W., 'Imperfect Reasons and Rational Options', *Noûs*, Vol. 46, No. 1 (February 2012): 24-60

Potter Nelson, 'The Argument of Kant's *Groundwork*, Chapter 1' in Paul Guyer (ed.), *Kant's Groundwork of the Metaphysics of Morals: Critical Essays* (Maryland: Rowman & Littlefield Publishers, Inc., 1998): 29-50

Potter, Nelson, 'Duties to Oneself, Motivational Internalism and Self-Deception in Kant's Ethics', in Mark Timmons (ed.), *Kant's Metaphysics of Morals: Interpretative Essays* (New York: Oxford University Press, 2002): 371-389

PwC (2017), *Talent Development*, http://www.pwc.com/us/en/hr-saratoga/talent-assessments.html, accessed 30.03.2017

Railton, Peter, 'Alienation, Consequentialism, and the Demands of Morality', *Philosophy and Public Affairs*, Vol. 13, No. 2 (Spring, 1984): 134-171

Railton, Peter, *Facts, Values and Norms: Essays Toward a Morality of Consequence* (Cambridge: Cambridge University Press, 2003)

Rainbolt, George, 'Perfect and Imperfect Obligations', *Philosophical Studies*, Vol. 98, No. 3 (April 2000): 233-256

Rawls, John, *Political Liberalism* (New York: Columbia University Press, 1993)

Rawls, John, *A Theory of Justice*, Revised Edition (Cambridge, MA: The Belknap Press of Harvard University Press, 1999)

Raz, Joseph, *The Morality of Freedom* (Oxford: Clarendon Press, 1986)

Raz, Joseph, *Practical Reason and Norms* (Oxford: Oxford University Press, 1999)

Raz, Joseph, *Engaging Reason: On the Theory of Value and Action* (Oxford: Oxford University Press, 2000)

Reath, Andrews 'Self-Legislation and Duties to Oneself' in Mark Timmons (ed.), *Kant's Metaphysics of Morals: Interpretative Essays* (New York: Oxford University Press, 2002): 351-370

Renzulli, J. S., 'The Three-Ring Conception of Giftedness: A Developmental Model for Promoting Creative Productivity', in Robert J. Sternberg & Janet E. Davidson (eds), *Conceptions of Giftedness*, Second Edition (Cambridge: Cambridge University Press, 2005): 246-279

Rivera, Lisa, 'Sacrifices, Aspirations and Morality: Williams Reconsidered', *Ethical Theory and Moral Practice*, Vol. 10, Issue 1 (February 2007): 69-87

Roemer E. John, 'A Pragmatic Theory of Responsibility for the Egalitarian Planner', *Philosophy and Public Affairs*, Vol. 22, No. 2 (Spring 1993): 146-166

Ronay, Barney, 'Brendan Rodgers is Misguided in Singling out Mario Balotelli for Criticism', *The Guardian* (23rd October 2014), https://www.theguardian.com/football/blog/2014/oct/23/brendan-rodgers-mario-balotelli-liverpool, accessed 01.12.2016

Rosati, Connie S., 'Person's, Perspectives and Full Information Accounts of the Good', *Ethics*, Vol. 105, No. 2 (January, 1995): 296-325

Rosati, Connie, 'Internalism and the Good for a Person', *Ethics*, Vol. 106, No. 2 (January 1996): 297-326

Rosati, Connie S., 'Preference-Formation and Personal Good', in Serena Olsaretti (ed.), *Preferences and Well-Being* (Cambridge: Cambridge University Press, 2006): 33-65

Ryle, Gilbert, *The Concept of Mind* (Oxford: Routledge, 2009)

Scanlon, Tim, *What we Owe to Each Other* (Cambridge, MA: Belknap Press of Harvard University Press, 1998)

Scheffler, Samuel, *Human Morality* (Oxford: Oxford University Press, 1992)

Scheffler, Samuel, *The Rejection of Consequentialism: A Philosophical Investigation of the Considerations of Underlying Rival Moral Conceptions* (Oxford: Oxford University Press, 1994)

Scheffler, Samuel, 'Choice, Circumstance, and the Value of Equality', *Politics, Philosophy, and Economics,* Vol. 4, No. 1 (2005): 5-28

Schemmel, Christian, 'Distributive and Relational Equality', *Politics, Philosophy and Economics,* Vol. 11, No. 2 (2011): 123-148

Schroeder, S. Andrew, 'Imperfect Duties, Group Obligations, and Beneficence', *Journal of Moral Philosophy,* Vol. 11, Issue 5 (2014): 557-584

Schwartz, Daniel, 'Luck and the Domain of Distributive Justice' *European Journal of Philosophy,* Vol. 18, No. 2 (2009): 244-261

Sedgwick, Sally, *Kant's Groundwork of the Metaphysics of Morals: An Introduction* (New York: Cambridge University Press, 2008)

Seel, Norbert M. (ed.), *Encyclopaedia of the Sciences of Learning* (New York: Springer, 2012)

Segall, Shlomi, *Equality and Opportunity* (Oxford: Oxford University Press, 2013)

Sen, Amartya K., *On Ethics and Economics* (Malden, MA/Oxford: Wiley-Blackwell, 1989)

Sher, George, 'Talents and Choices' *Noûs,* Vol. 46, Issue 3 (2012): 400-417

Sin, William, 'Internalization and Moral Demands', *Philosophical Studies,* Vol. 153, No. 2 (2012): 163-175

Singer, M. G., 'On Duties to Oneself', *Ethics,* Vol. 69, No. 3 (April 1959): 202-205

Singer, Peter, *Practical Ethics* (Cambridge: Cambridge University Press, 1993)

Sloboda, John A., Davidson, Jane W., Howe, Michael J. A., & Moore, Derek G., 'The Role of Practice in the Development of Performing Musicians', *British Journal of Psychology,* Vol. 87, No. 2 (May 1996): 287-309

Sloboda, John A., & Howe, Michael J. A., 'Musical Talent and Individual Differences in Musical Achievement: A Reply to Gagné', *Psychology of Music*, Vol. 27, No. 1 (April 1999): 52-54

Slote, Michael, *The Ethics of Care and Empathy* (New York/Oxford: Routledge, 2007)

Slote, Michael, *Education and Human Values: Reconciling Talent with an Ethics of Care* (New York/Oxford: Routledge, 2012)

Snodgrass, Klyne, *Stories with Intent: A Comprehensive Guide to the Parables of Jesus* (Grand Rapids, Michigan/Cambridge UK: William B. Eerdmans Publishing Company, 2008)

Sobel, David, 'Full Information Accounts of Well-Being', *Ethics*, Vol. 104, No. 4 (1994): 784-810

Sobel, David, 'Subjective Accounts of Reasons for Action', *Ethics* 111, No. 3 (April, 2001): 461-492

Sobel, David, 'The Impotence of the Demandingness Objection', *Philosophers' Imprint*, Vol. 7, No. 8 (September 2007): 1-17

Sobel, David, 'Subjectivism and Idealization', *Ethics*, Vol. 119, No. 2 (January, 2009): 336-352

Sorrell, Tom, 'Morality and Emergency', *Proceedings of the Aristotelian Society*, New Series, Vol. 103 (2003): 21-37

Spector, Ezequiel, 'Do You Deserve to be Talented?', *Utilitas*, Vol. 23, No. 1 (March 2011): 115-125

Sport Scotland (2013), *Understanding Talent*, https://www.youtube.com/watch?v=LfUvchfrcS0, accessed 01/12/2016

Sternberg, Robert J., & Davidson, Janet E., 'Conceptions of Giftedness: A Map of the Terrain', in Robert J. Sternberg & Janet E. Davidson (eds), *Conceptions of Giftedness* (New York: Cambridge University Press, 1986): 3-18

Sternberg, Robert J., & Zhang, Li-fang, 'What do We Mean by Giftedness? A Pentagonal Implicit Theory', *Gifted Child Quarterly*, Vol. 39, Issue 2 (1995): 88-94

Stocker, Michael, 'Acts, Perfect Duties and Imperfect Duties', *The Review of Metaphysics*, Vol. 20, No. 3 (March 1967): 207-217

Stroud, Sarah, 'Moral Overridingness and Moral Theory', *Pacific Philosophical Quarterly*, Vol. 79, No. 2 (June 1998): 170-186

Sumner, L. W., *Welfare, Happiness and Ethics* (Oxford: Oxford University Press, 1996)

Tan, Kok-Char, *Justice, Institutions, and Luck: The Site, Ground, and Scope of Equality* (Oxford: Oxford University Press, 2012)

Tiffany, Evan, 'Alienation and Internal Reasons for Action', *Social Theory and Practice*, Vol. 29, No. 3 (July 2003): 387-418

Timmerman, Jens, *Kant's Groundwork of the Metaphysical of Morals: A Commentary* (New York: Cambridge University Press, 2007)

Trehub, Sandra E., & Shellenberg, Glenn, 'Cultural Determinism is no Better than Biological Determinism', *Behavioral and Brain Sciences*, Vol. 21, No. 3 (1998): 428

UK Sport (2015), *Talent ID*, http://www.uksport.gov.uk/our-work/talent-id, accessed 20.03.2017

Van Ackeren, Marcel, and Sticker, Martin 'Kant and Moral Demandingness', *Ethical Theory and moral Practice*, Vol. 18, No. 1 (2015): 75-89

Viens, A. M., & Selgelid, Michael J., *Emergency Ethics* (Oxford: Routledge, 2012)

Voorhoeve, Alex, 'May a Government Mandate more Comprehensive Health Insurance than Citizens want for Themselves?' in David Sobel, Peter Vallentyne and Steven Wall (eds.), *Oxford Studies in Political Philosophy, Vol. 4* (Oxford: Oxford University Press, forthcoming)

Wall, Steven, *Liberalism, Perfectionism and Restraint* (Cambridge: Cambridge University Press, 1998)

Walla, Alice Pinheiro, 'Kant's Moral Theory and Demandingness', *Ethical Theory and Moral Practice*, Vol. 18 (2015): 731-743

Weinhold, Bob, 'Epigenetics: The Science of Change', *Environmental Health Perspectives*, Vol. 114, No. 3 (March 2006): A160-A167

Wilkinson, T. M., 'Against Dworkin's Endorsement Constraint', *Utilitas,* Vol. 15, No. 2 (July 2003): 175-193

Williams, Bernard, *Utilitarianism: For and Against* (Cambridge: Cambridge University Press, 1973)

Williams, Bernard, 'Utilitarianism and Moral Self-Indulgence' in Bernard Williams, *Moral Luck* (Cambridge: Cambridge University Press, 1981): 40-53

Williams, Bernard, *Ethics and the Limits of Morality* (New York/Oxford: Routledge, 2006)

Winner, Ellen, 'Talent: Don't Confuse Necessity with Sufficiency, or Science with Policy', *Behavioral and Brain Sciences,* Vol. 21, No. 3 (1998): 430-431

Winner, Ellen, 'Giftedness: Current Theory and Research', *Current Directions in Psychological Science,* Vol. 9, No. 5 (October 2000): 153-156

Wolf, Susan, 'Moral Saints', *The Journal of Philosophy*, Vol. 79, No. 8 (August, 1982): 419-439

Wolff, Jonathan, 'Fairness, Respect, and the Egalitarian Ethos, *Philosophy and Public Affairs*, Vol. 27, No. 2 (Spring 1998): 97-12

Yelle, Benjamin, 'Alienation, Deprivation, and the Well-being of Persons', *Utilitas*, Vol. 26, No. 4 (December 2014): 367-384

Zagzebski, Linda Trinkaus, *Virtue of the Mind: An Inquiry into the Nature of Virtue and the Ethical Foundations of Knowledge* (Cambridge: Cambridge University Press, 1996)